THE WIG

THE
WIG
A
Hairbrained
History

LUIGI AMARA

Translated by Christina MacSweeney

REAKTION BOOKS

Published by
REAKTION BOOKS LTD
Unit 32, Waterside
44–48 Wharf Road
London N1 7UX, UK

www.reaktionbooks.co.uk

First published in English 2020
English-language translation copyright © Reaktion Books 2020
Translated by Christina MacSweeney

Copyright © Luigi Amara 2014
Originally published by Editorial Anagrama SA
c/o Indent Literary Agency LLC

This publication was made possible by the Secretaría de Cultura
of the Mexican Government, via the Fondo Nacional para la
Cultura y las Artes, with a grant from the Literary Translation
Program (PROTRAD)

Printed and bound in Malta by Gutenberg Press Ltd

A catalogue record for this book is available from the British Library

ISBN 978 1 78914 346 1

Contents

*In tragic desperation, he brutally tore out
the hair of his wig.*

Carlos Díaz Dufoo Jr

An Otherworldly Prologue

If I had to decide on an object to describe the meaning of life on Earth, a postcard to send to Mars about our most dearly held obsessions, my first choice would be the wig. Mammalian yet artificial, an insignia of power and, at the same time, complicit in a malleable, remote but enduring notion of beauty; reflected in the false head of hair – apparently en route to a life of its own – are our excesses and fears, the deployment of the body for purposes of seduction, plus the psychological traumas of that simulacrum of autumn known as baldness.

For all that it reveals of our propensity for duplicity and simulation, for the way in which it crystallizes – in a tangled mesh that somehow seems to be ready to both pounce and caress – the deviation and concerted exuberance of that world within the world we have agreed to call 'second nature' (but could also be termed 'theatre'); for all those reasons, I would choose the wig as our sidereal representative, as a cosmic calling card. I like to imagine the wig crossing the indifference of space and, after many years, arriving in another galaxy; I like to imagine the amazement of some extraterrestrial being holding in its hands, in its perhaps smooth, horrified extremities, that light, crouching mat of hair that, while perhaps indecipherable, speaks of a hirsute, stylized world where nothing is what it seems, and while attenuated (possibly due to its participation in a primary need, in the unsilenceable demands of desire) is still convincing.

More than an illustrated and, it has to be said, slightly disjointed history of the mania for hairpieces – a sort of reflective mosaic or tapestry of a topic one might describe as outmoded – this is a personal book, an intimate, possibly overly insistent gallery surrounding a single object. Rather than a horizontal museum, a motley collection of recurrent weaknesses and fetishes, and making light of the risk of the monomania and anachronism involved, I opted for a journey into the interior of one of those recurrences, a descent down the plait of associations and perplexities in which I see myself reflected when I meditate on the wig, when I allow myself to become entangled in its incitements, in its improbable density, while converting it into an object of thought. And in the end, if Baudelaire discovered there is a whole world in a head of hair, why not go one step further and tell the story of the world in terms of the wig, in terms of the hair that stands alone, detached from the shaggy hide, and thus the body; in terms of the head of hair elevated to a talisman, a small but vast cosmos?

Although this is, in some way, an autobiographical book, its germ is not, as far as I know – one should not pass up the opportunity of a nod to the psychoanalyst – to be found in any shameful paraphilia or a more or less controlled, more or less domesticated propensity for cross-dressing. Neither did it have its origin – although this must in some way have been involved – in reading the epigram by Carlos Díaz Dufoo Jr I have used as a sort of epigraph, an authentic one-line novel to which these pages may be nothing more than a rather bulky footnote, an offcut that is possibly as unwarranted as it is redundant. I suspect this book in fact began when long hair was still fashionable, in those not-so-distant times when one's locks could be a symbol of rebellion. One evening I realized that if we find liberating qualities in long, loose hair, or a certain stridency in dyeing it green and moulding it à la barbed wire, the wig introduces an unexpected distortion, an ambiguity that makes incursions into the province of disguise: beyond fashion and the codes of cosmetics, the wig embodies the paradox of a portable, detachable freedom, of a, one could say, two-faced rebellion – festive and extraordinary due to its carnivalesque aura – no less destabilizing for being removable.

Alongside its antecedents – only in appearance frivolous – in the old French salons, I noted that the wig was more suited to the profligacy of licentious nights than to freedom as a revolutionary value and, attracted by its artifice, the fascination of its deceptive superficiality, I began to wonder if the symbolic importance of the guillotine during the French Revolution might be that it did away in one stroke with the reign of wigs; that, under the somewhat drastic pretext of decapitation, it put an end to those outlandish crests that could scarcely dissimulate their condition as crowns, and which, for a couple of centuries, dominated social life, just as they had in ancient Egypt.

On that day, I fell under the spell of the wig, and cherished the hope of writing a book that, in addition to leading me to examine the customs of a variety of different eras, would oblige me to reflect on a strange presence, generally disdained as superfluous, and unconditionally expelled from the realm of the thinkable. A language in itself, a complement of the mask made from the very material of our own sebaceous glands, an identity toy, the wig is usually marginalized by 'serious' research projects – despite the fact that the first known one dates from 3000 BC, and that at certain moments in history it spread like a hydra, the number of whose heads corresponded to those of the population who gladly donned it – even those dealing with the alterations to which the body is subjected, those that investigate the boundaries between the organic and the synthetic, the carnal and the prosthetic, what is original to the human species and what is added.

If one of the key questions of modernity was related to the validity of the conception of the mind as a blank sheet, an unmarked surface without predispositions or impressions, it is hardly surprising that, in relation to one of the principal problems of thought, the host of philosophers of those elegant,

Wig found in the inner coffin of Queen Meritamun, wife of Pharaoh Ramesses the Great, c. 1040–992 BC. It is made of braids of human hair fastened at the top with a cord.

optimistic times (all under the effects of the fever for false hair, the distinction of capillary laurels dusted with white powder) did not extend their research to the body itself – the other, now scandalous, half of the dualism – and, in spite of the exaggerated evidence resting on their heads, agreed on its neutrality, on its condition as a mere datum, as if the body could be on the margins of the inscriptions of power, and free from symbolic imprints, the configurations of language, and even collective ailments.

As there is now practically no doubt that we live in the age of the cyborg, in a time open to ambiguity and the reinvention of the human in which technology constantly violates the frontiers between the biological and the artificial, between nature and culture, the personal and the other, I thought I perceived in the wig – in that network of hair and ritual practices committed to making an impression – a perhaps archaic, perhaps embryonic, but ultimately valiant and suggestive antecedent to ways of overcoming the limitations of the body, and to altering the possibilities of identity. Just as in the fleeting frame of a wig party – the contemporary, if somewhat diminished version of the old Roman celebrations, where social roles were exchanged, and women often covered themselves in the skins of wild beasts – the visage displaced by a hairpiece becomes something other, something we hide behind when representing ourselves to the world, but through which we simultaneously project ourselves. So, perhaps, the primitive custom of wearing wigs in time led to a reconsideration of the body as an unquestioned inheritance, and paved the way for the induced metamorphosis, for that subversion of the given, of what presents itself as inalterable in sexual politics or what we accept as human.

Maybe all this sounds a little out of this world, but that conjectured gift to Mars with which I opened these pages, that coquettish mass of hair travelling to the edges of the Milky Way in search of a radical other with which to confront us, is possibly one of the first symbols of our mutation as a species. It is a glimmer – no matter how passing or easily disassembled – of the power to have an influence over ourselves, to change the course of clearly unalterable things, of all that presents itself as fate, as a touchstone leaving room only for resignation, and not, for example, creativity or expressive intervention.

While I contemplate the imaginary flight of the wig through the firmament and watch how its trail crosses the starry night to one side of its celestial twin – the tresses of the constellation of Coma Berenices – I cannot help but think that this age-old accessory, this uncertain article so often accused of falsity, ridiculousness and injustice, this rarefication of our primate charms, was a rudimentary link in the long process of extending human life beyond its limits, beyond its apparently fixed, stable, sacrosanct forms. Even before the first glimpses of the 'Smart Wig' (an apparatus already under patent, combining an instrument for navigation, a terminal for instant medical analyses, a bundle of threadlike sensors and a portable communications interface), the old-fashioned, blatantly obvious wig, which at its zenith was made from a quantity of hair no human head could ever produce unaided, had already set humanity on the road to its self-transformation; it had already questioned from the only possible position (from the zone of appearance, dismissed as dispensable and futile, in which effects reign) the location of essentialist notions of identity, gender and the body.

A Theory of Disguise

A recurrent accessory of deception, the perfect means for passing unnoticed, the wig is a ruse capable of throwing even the person wearing it off track. Hair, which can be on the side of either beauty or concealment, is the most malleable part of the body and, on the wheel of fortune of its mutations, compromises not only our appearance, but the very notion of who we are. According to anthropological theory, the human face lost its hair over millennia, so enabling it to be read. Once muscle activity became a source of signals, an authentic language, it was only to be expected that hair – in the form of attachments and wigs, understood as cloaks or cowls – would return to the face with the intention of causing confusion.

To make Wakefield's case of 'marital delinquency' less whimsical, in his eponymous short story of 1835, Nathaniel Hawthorne imagines him in a wig shop. Wakefield doesn't know if his resolve not to return home is a short-lived act of waywardness or a twenty-year period of voluntary exile, but he takes the precaution of changing his appearance: he dresses in the discreet second-hand clothing of a Jew and buys a reddish head of hair that in many cities would have attracted attention, but in the patchwork of colours that is London has the effect of producing invisibility. (Around the same time, Edgar Allan Poe was positing the audacious theory that the best way to make something disappear was to leave it where anyone can see it.) Even though he has only moved a few metres from his wife – unsure whether or not to accept that she is a widow – thanks to what could be thought of as a superficial transformation, instead of living in the shadows, the self-exiled Wakefield transforms himself into another individual. Not even on the afternoon when, in the urban bustle, the stream of humanity forces the couple into proximity, and even perilous momentary contact, is the spell of his anonymity broken.

As Hawthorne notes, it is likely that in the long joke of living in the margins, Wakefield's vanity plays an important part – the morbid, possibly pathological curiosity to see how the world will fare without him. In time, nevertheless, the mask will become the face of the cloaked body and it is not unthinkable that, on waking, in the instant of shock at the sight of his wig-less self, Wakefield would believe he had surprised an imposter.

Constructed in part before the mirror of others, chiselled each day with the points of intersection in how they see us, cosmetic changes are also part of the image we form of ourselves, erasing on our own faces the frontiers of the proper and improper. If, in addition to expressing our personalities, clothes and hairstyles allow us to approach what we suspect or imagine ourselves to be, then fitting a wig or doing our make-up, more than the artifices of simulation or duplicity, are aspects of an everyday ritual of restitution.

During the secret, melancholic saturnalias when he drunk himself under the bedside table, Wakefield altered his appearance in order to disappear, but also with an arduous commitment to reinventing himself. Once busy, egoistic London had confirmed that – however eccentric his plan – he had become nobody, he was able to evolve as naturally as a ghost. What had started as a tangential game ultimately brought about his inner conversion, to the point where, for a long time, he had no idea how to reverse the process. His odyssey around the corner took as long as that of Ulysses, 'the man of twists and turns', the peerless imposter. Wakefield also returned home twenty years later, like someone coming back from a parallel world, casting off his disguise. But before converting himself back into Wakefield, thanks to the alteration of one of the most striking – and, significantly, the one he could most easily live without – parts of his body, he discovered that not only the form of the face can be manipulated, but also the personality.

When the fatwa was pronounced against Salman Rushdie in 1989, the recommendation of the London Metropolitan Police seemed inspired by Wakefield and Poe's detective brain: covering the face would attract immediate attention, so the best thing to do was leave it uncovered, and trust in the powers of the wig, just as highwaymen and such generals of military campaigns as Hannibal Barca had done in bygone days. Instead of hiding in a bunker, he would be able to walk merrily through the streets as if the harassment for insulting the name of God belonged to a past era. The police, on the side of the economy of disguise – it is enough to alter the most decisive features to become unrecognizable – did not take into account that rather than just disguising a man, their mission consisted of wiping out all trace of a figurehead, an unexpected symbol.

The police also insisted he adopt an alias; so he could at least sign cheques without endangering his life. The sorcery of words was more powerful than the capillary mystification; Rushdie – a thoroughbred writer, even in hiding – not only changed his name, but took on his new identity with the will of a fictitious character. When it came to writing about those blasphemous years as Joseph Anton – a perhaps rather obvious tribute to his favourite authors, Joseph Conrad and Anton Chekhov – Rushdie chose to use the third-person singular, as if he were really narrating the story of another man, someone who is not, was not, him.

Despite the fact that there is no wig capable of concealing an emblem or distracting fanaticism, the failure of Rushdie's hairpiece can perhaps be put down to his own disbelief. Instead of seeing the disguise as the first stage of metamorphosis, he made the common mistake of thinking of it as a veil, a screen. Already over forty years old, his forehead had set out to extend

The Chimerical Gift, 2011. 'The wig was made and arrived in a brown cardboard box looking like a small sleeping animal,' Salman Rushdie, *Joseph Anton: A Memoir* (2012).

its dominions into new hemispheres, and the interference of a certain inconsistent, juvenile pride cannot be discounted. When he opened the box containing the wig – made to replicate the texture of his own hair and match his complexion – he thought he saw a small, sleeping animal. How could he become someone else if he was afraid of looking like Daniel Boone? On a trial walk down Loane Street, laughter was not long in coming. The last straw was when someone shouted: 'Look, there's that bastard Rushdie in a wig!'

It is said that Menephron was one of the freest of men since, having on no occasion come across water calm enough to give him even a brief glimpse of his features, he never saw the reflection of his face. Wakefield, who looked at himself every day in the mirror to live up to his disguise, knew the freedom of one who has temporarily renounced his face, that spurious freedom of the person who, still attached to the world, can no longer participate in it. During the period when he bifurcated into Joseph Anton, Rushdie had first-hand experience of what he had so often achieved in his writing, but he never succeeded in inventing a new face for himself. At the cost of his freedom, he etched his features onto the other into whom he should have changed, conferred on that other his stubborn, usual appearance – which, it would seem, he was unwilling to give up. During his terrible years in hiding, while the fanatical threat still hung over him, there were two men with the same face, the face of a wanted man.

Casanova, Wigs and Masks

The notion of hair as a vital force, or baldness as an indication of abundant androgens, cedes before the elusive, operatic print of Casanova wearing a wig. In the very middle of that old dispute dividing the male gender – about which women believe they always have the last word – the libertine tiptoes along like a sly, dissolute Moses, having put a centre parting in the choppy waters of the discussion.

With a refinement evocative of a masked ball – aided by a *mise en scène* that invites both the stolen kiss and slapstick comedy – and light-footed in spite of carrying on his shoulders the saturation of Rococo, Casanova, swathed in a cape reminiscent of death (and only afterwards love), bursts into the room and adjourns the debate. His scarlet splendour, his elegance mottled with errors (who can present himself as a lover without vacillation and babbling?), his prosaic opportunism and his gallant persistence, which neither excludes weeping nor fears seeming ridiculous, would all be little help in winning over women if they were not part of an intricate pantomime, a slow, prearranged dance in which, over and above the sincerity or otherwise of the feelings, what is decisive is the mask, the theatricality of the seduction.

If the idea of apocryphal hair as an aphrodisiac now seems unlikely, it is because we forget the charm of eighteenth-century imposture. Changing identity at every carnival period, passing for someone else – a candid aristocrat or devilish priest – or, better still, allowing others to be carried away by the tide of doubt and the spell, is already putting one foot on the slope, on the inclined plane, of transgression.

In any re-evaluation of Casanova, it is impossible to over-emphasize the fact that he belonged to an acting family, and felt at ease among con artists. Although his claims to nobility were pulled from his lace-edged sleeve, that does not make them less valid, or mean he was intimidated by the possibility that he might not be able to fill the role. After all, however more differentiated society was at that time, it was also more permissive and welcoming; it favoured internal mobility, meteoric ascents and plummeting falls into ruin: successive waves of glory and scandal. In the highly stratified but porous edifice of the Baroque, a person without a homeland or ancestry could very well find an entrance into salons and boudoirs – even reach the throne – based on his self-esteem and appearance, while others, despite titles and high position, fell into the abyss of dishonour, or ended up in prison. Fortune was perhaps at its most fickle, and it was necessary to adapt to so much ephemerality and inconsistency.

If everything in love is ambience and propitious occasion, a conspiratorial alignment of favourable elements (beginning with the stagnant, intimate Venice, a city that regularly presents lovers with the first, most difficult of steps: availability and ambiguity), in the theatrical logic of Giacomo Casanova one must not only create very different characters, but do so with equal care and unscrupulousness, like someone who skilfully deals with obstacles and ambushes in a sporting spirit. It is not that one has to disguise oneself as a monk in order to worm one's

'A Wigmaker-barber Shop', by R. Bénard, after J. R. Lucotte, engraving in D. Diderot and J. le Rond d'Alembert, *Recueil de planches, sur les sciences et les arts* (1771).

way into a damsel's bedroom; for a time one *is* the monk. But Casanova's dedication – his vocation? – suspends disbelief, so there will be no great difficulty in reinventing himself later, with all the appropriate paraphernalia, as a soldier or violinist, a lawyer or doctor, a cabalist or gambler, and, finally, as a relic of a long-buried era, in the languid, pitiful role of one who resigns himself, once over the hill of euphoria and diversion, to simple memory and writing.

If masks create favourable conditions for entanglement, they also lead to an acceptance of internal tensions. Changeable and interstitial, the sham Chevalier de Seingalt is a talented foreigner; since his notion of adventure embraces both scepticism and setbacks, he has shed the pathos of gravity, allowing him to slip through the palaces, dungeons, bedrooms and theatre boxes of Europe with the volatility and passion of one who understands that the comedy has to be played out to the end. The opposite of a trophy-collecting Don Juan with his compendium of deeply disturbing falsities, Casanova arranges matters so that he gives himself body and soul to each and every one of his innumerable conquests. He is much more than an itinerant actor: he is a full-time thespian with a talent for farce and improvisation who knows, as so few do, how to make the mask into a festive likeness of the soul.

He would frequently go about masked, even when the carnival period was not at hand. In contrast to the ordinary facial disguises – composed of false hair, velvet and ingenuity – that opened the doors to palaces, women's legs and the arms of the Pope himself, the Venetian variety allowed him to flee from the character of the moment, in order to commit acts of villainy and rowdiness, to take his revenge on a rival with a thrashing (in ancient Rome, Nero wore wigs to beat up strangers and so enjoy, at his ease, the pleasure of the arbitrary). If a masked presence contains something of an emissary of death, the simple gesture of wearing a face covering makes the visage into a skull and the skin bone. Layered like a set of Russian dolls, beneath that first mask – that we agree to call *persona* – there is only another mask, and another, all worn (if it is not redundant to say so) with versatile nihilism.

With his trickster's skill and his genius for kitsch special effects, Casanova postulates that if one wants to prosper in the theatre of the world, if one wants to arouse the opposite sex, the void must be disguised. True, he never repents anything, and recalls his long string of deceit with a wealth of detail and astonishing delight; but this is not cynicism: circumstances force him to make each role his own, to play the game through. Life is not a dream, it is theatre, and there is never enough time to rehearse.

It is no surprise that, for someone who doesn't consider the possibility of lulls in the performance, of a backstage behind the artifice, the naked body is a superstition, a cast-off without charm, fertile ground for venereal disease and parasites. A lack of cosmetics and clothing is not only an ephemeral, sometimes uncomfortable and degrading bodily condition, but also reduces that body to anatomy, an inelegant collection of organs determined to decorously fulfil their functions. For Venus' intrepid lackey, the body present in the act of falling in love – perhaps the phrase most resistant to interpretation, but so often repeated in *The Story of My Life* – is that slightly abstract and imaginary body, glimpsed beneath a skirt, or about to over-flow a neckline.

The wig, a crucial element of his wardrobe – one might say his psychology – fell on his head very early on, when he was still a child and had to have his louse-ridden scalp shaved. After that, his appearance passed through more phases than the Moon, and from the tonsure to flowing tresses, from outlandish coiffures to pigtails, via multiple models of wig, his grooming of his locks would be so ostentatious and fantastical that, on a certain occasion, a priest censured him, saying that 'the Devil had caught him by the hair.'

One of his most fervent readers, the author Miklós Szentkuthy – lover of unreality and the orgy, who dreamed of bringing together his complete works under the amusingly bare-faced title of *Self-portraits with a Mask* – liked to don a white wig, with long tubular curls over the ears and a hairy frontal mound, in order

'Casanova and the Condom' (1872), illustration from an edition of Casanova's autobiography published in Brussels depicting Casanova at the age of thirty in Switzerland.

to dress up as Casanova, so far did he share the Venetian's delight in licentiousness, mannerism and its strange metaphysics.

For Szentkuthy, as with any hangover baroque figure who fits Casanovan props to his body, the mass of hair doesn't work the miracle of converting him into a gallant, but shows that the wig alone, while leaving the features open to view, is a kind of mask, a toy of the ego, that both facilitates the development of a character and assists in overcoming inhibitions. The face can still give us away, but the new appearance, bordering on the frontiers of what is illicit and eccentric, induces unusual forms of behaviour, creates an atmosphere in which sensuality lets down its hair and gives itself up to misconduct. Rather than a mechanism of concealment, the wig is a mental mask, an entry into metamorphosis, an invisible, paradoxical veil that excites us to reinvent ourselves, to recover from a snub, and try again.

Freed from the uncomfortable burden of morality, Casanova wasn't the sort to give lectures. But from among the many things that can be inferred from his memoir, I have picked out the following, referring to the utility of the wig in the realm of Cupid: with the identity scrambled and deprived of its weightiness by a touch of fantasy, by that facial hiatus that takes us (however slightly) out of ourselves, in a state propitious to committing acts of madness, it is only necessary to add the well-known formulas of love – the arsenal of phrases, stiff as a board, but slicked with the brilliantine of the day – to complete the conquest.

The She-wolf of the Night: Messalina

Messalina was reclining, waiting for her husband, Emperor Claudius, to fall asleep so she could escape from the marriage bed to the *lupanar*. Concealed beneath a cloak, she would pass through the streets of Rome until she reached the red-light district of Suburra on the outskirts of the city. During this journey, a fiery wig completed her transformation: she left behind the empress, the omnipotent matron with thick black hair, to become the *meretrix augusta*, as Juvenal's spiteful poem describes her. Everyone in the brothel knows her as Licisca, a Greek word meaning 'she-wolf cub', used to name female canines. There, in a steamy room, her eyes embellished with antimony, lips exaggeratedly vermilion, she would uncover her breasts, dusted in gold, and, of course, charge for her services.

Valeria Messalina – the adolescent empress in wolf's clothing, the barbarian who invoked disorder in the bosom of civilization – used wigs not as a disguise but as a symbol: for her they were a propitiatory rite. In Rome, where apparel was regulated, prostitutes were obliged to dye their hair or wear a blonde wig as a distinctive mark; Messalina's wigs were, apparently, reddish, with a hint of saffron, a sign that she did not earn her living by selling her body, but rather bought her freedom by its sale on the matting of the brothel floor.

On the occasions when, returning to the Palatine Hill, 'tired of men but not satiated yet', she found she had forgotten her transformative mane, it was invariably returned to her – still reeking of the *lupanar* and sex – as everyone was aware that without it, without the wig that enabled her to let her hair down, the duplicitous, unstable Messalina, the versatile empress of the dark piercing gaze, the bored child consort in the centre of the world, would feel incomplete, in some way divided in two.*

Her ambition and sexual drive were so astonishing that she entered the dictionary as a noun referring to a dominant, dissolute woman. Otherwise, she had two great passions: gardening and the senator Gaius Silius – 'the most beautiful of Roman youths', according to Tacitus. These two passions coincided in her final hours. Naturally, she didn't love Claudius; the self-proclaimed god was much older than her, had a stammer and a hunchback, and was a focus of antagonism. Once she had given him children and, more importantly, a legitimate candidate for the throne (Britannicus, whom Nero later had poisoned), Messalina gave herself up to infidelity. She was very young, provocative, worshipped the god Priapus – to whom she made constant offerings of myrtle wreaths – and was as beautiful as the softness of her name would suggest.

~~~~

* The detail of the return of the wig should perhaps be understood as a wink that, nevertheless, does not exclude the elegance of tacit censure: in fact, Messalina had a formidable arsenal of wigs – around four hundred – and the loss of one would not have compromised her escapades. (Although this is a considerable quantity, it hardly bears comparison with the number another celebrated empress boasted of in her passion for hairpieces: the collection of Faustina the Elder, wife of Antoninus Pius, contained approximately seven hundred, of different colours, sizes and styles.)

It is supposed that she was a nymphomaniac, 'equally capricious in her passions and dislikes', and nineteenth-century physiognomists did not hesitate to place her in the shameful category of the 'criminal female'. There are any number of suggestions – some written in unparalleled hexameters – that she slept with literally every man in Rome. By the year 45 BC, all roads led to her cubicle, the small space reserved for her in the brothel. Gladiators and nobles, guards and conspirators, soldiers and consuls, anyone could satisfy their dreams of grandeur in the arms of the bitch-empress, whose image was reproduced on coins and as statues throughout civilization, always with chaste coiffures that restrained her hair and were the emblem of her honour. Half the world knew that on the reverse of the coin Messalina was wearing a wig and, victim to continual arousal (*rigida volva*), renounced the marmoreal role her position bound her to and laughed at her duties as a matron, casting off the dress and mantle (*stolla* and *palla*) that marked her as a sacrosanct Roman citizen. According to some, she made frequent use of threats and tortuous intrigues to obtain the favours of those who resisted her for fear of reprisal. She was always the last to leave the *lupanar*.

Yet if there was a period when it was impossible to pronounce her name without raising scandal, this was not due to her wigs or uncontrolled libido. In those times, the word 'adultery' could be a way of referring to political astuteness, and it should not be forgotten that her antecedents on the throne (the Julias, Livias and Agrippinas) acted no differently, making the marriage bed one of the natural seats of intrigue. As Pascal Quignard points out in *Sex and Terror* – and before him Heinrich Stadelmann – Messalina's true immorality was to have fallen madly in love with Silius, an unpardonable fault in a woman of her rank, not so much because she was already married as because that emotion located her in the delicate position of servitude.

While she was a she-wolf by night, organizing championships of amatory stamina with the prostitutes and leading a double life thanks to the enchantment of her wig, she had no impact on the most sacred area of Roman life: the future of the imperial dynasty. But love; that upset the apple cart. Or such was the view of Tacitus (*Annals*, XI, 28), who in the face of prudish interpretations of the criminal rage her shameless marriage to Silius triggered in Claudius, wrote: 'While Messalina industriously hid her adultery in the cloaca of the prince there was dishonour of the truth, but no danger.'

The peril lay in her love, in what it might awaken beyond her wig games: in giving herself up to another man to the absurd point of marrying him, thus compromising the lineage and the

Hans Makart, *Charlotte Wolter as Messalina*, c. 1875, oil on canvas.

Belinda Lee in the role of Messalina, the eponymous character in the 1960 film directed by Vittorio Cottafavi.

empire. After the wedding, the Bacchanal of the autumn grape harvest was celebrated and Messalina – drunk, her hair loose (*crine fluxo*) and one breast bared to play the role of Ariadne – heard news of approaching vengeance. The shrewd empress, supreme in the arts of deception and disguise, had managed to persuade Claudius that the marriage was a sham and had, incredibly, gained his consent for it. But many others understood the new marriage as a slap in the face of the empire, and convinced Claudius to immediately have her executed, not allowing her the chance to wind him round her little finger once again.

Death came to her in her favourite place: the house of pleasure in the Gardens of Lucullus. According to some versions, she wrote another letter to Claudius. On discovering that his executioners were approaching, she unsuccessfully attempted to

31

commit suicide with her pen (*stilus*). A guard plunged his sword into her breast. Very soon afterwards, the order was given to destroy every single statue of her. She was 23 years old.

In spite of the fact that it is not to be found in the pages of Tacitus or Pliny the Elder, nor in Juvenal or Cassius Dio, it is not difficult to imagine the scene in which Claudius goes to Suburra and, in disguise, making an effort to dissimulate his limp, without once opening his mouth so as not to reveal his stammer, joins the line in the brothel to lie with the peerless Licisca, the beautiful, slender stranger with whom he slept every night.

The Rage Called Wig

As often happens with great revolutions in fashion, the empire of the wig was established more by chance than design or ingenuity, and if half the populations of France and England in a particular period began the day by donning a head of false hair, this is in great part due to the fact that vanity, chance and even the anomalies of the body are hidden mechanisms in the motor of history. 'Many surprising fashions in dress have arisen from the fact that a famous man or woman tried to conceal some infirmity,' wrote Jean Cocteau, in a statement that could be seen as an apposite description of the capillary excesses of the seventeenth century, when, for the first time since ancient Egypt, men were infected with the passion for sham hair and women flaunted coiffures so high and prolific that stuffed birds nested in them.

Although Louis XIII's premature baldness stands out as the root cause of a renaissance of the wig that extended over almost two centuries – until its symbolic ending in the French Revolution – already, in 1620, Abbé de la Rivière had been greeted with an ovation when he appeared in court with a resplendent model that reached to his waist. Travellers had previously mentioned the enthusiasm in Paris for an eccentricity named *perruque*, which was an audacious solution to the age-old problem of depopulated pates. But once the king began to sport an asymmetric variety – the left side was longer than the right – the wig spread like a plague of mystifications, first among the court and gradually as an emblem of the professional classes; in spite of the high production costs and their supposed link to migraines, vertigo, hives and apoplexy, very soon all and sundry – from servants to the clergy, and even children – were wearing perukes, and in certain spheres a refusal to do so was considered as stubborn and ridiculous as spurning trousers would be nowadays. The Royal House of France employed 48 master craftsmen to meet the needs of Versailles, and the nascent guild of barber-wigmakers – whose sharpened instruments were no longer used in operations of a surgical nature and which, a century later, would have over a thousand members in Paris alone – became so honourable that one of its most celebrated members, *maître* André, believed he had the right to correspond with Voltaire on equal terms.[*]

How was it that an improbable tangle of hair rose to the heights of being a byword for breeding and sophistication? What form of imitative process was at work for the wig to become a common necessity and not just the badge of the aristocracy? In the past, emperors and queens had used them without unleashing such a fever, and if the custom of borrowed hair had spread due to climatic conditions (by the time that Nefertiti's pathological baldness obliged her to use hairpieces, Egyptians had for a long while been shaving their heads to combat the

---

[*] In 1760, André Charles, master wigmaker, wrote a tragedy and boldly sent it to Voltaire. The philosopher replied with a single, now famous piece of advice, repeated a thousand times over four pages: 'Master André, make wigs, always wigs, nothing but wigs . . .'

heat, thus assigning the wig a place in social life), or could be understood as a caste attribute or patrician insignia (in Rome, they were worn by certain empresses and such emperors as Nero, Caligula, Domitian and Otho), never before had the fashion become so widespread that it seemed the whole world was imitating the king.

While in other times the wig had a tyrannical presence, like a fiscal measure for converting the spontaneous fruit of the follicles into riches, in the seventeenth century the equation was modified to the extent that the wig, converted into an object of desire and fascination, was able to shrug off the vulgarity of a decree. According to Dr Akerlio, in the middle of the fourth century BC, Mausolus, the ruler of Caria, decided to replenish his impoverished treasury with a never-before-seen endowment of wigs, only to then, when the moment was right, publish an edict making it obligatory for his subjects, regardless of age, gender or social position, to shave their heads. When the wigs appeared for sale, the whole population was forced by law to buy them at incredible prices and, moreover, thank their sovereign for his foresight. It is no surprise that Mausolus gave negative connotations to the word 'satrap', even if one of the Seven Wonders of the World was erected in his honour.

Despite such ploys, and while the wig still functioned as a symbol of noble pedigree, in the mid-seventeenth century people of all classes were flocking to adopt some form of hairpiece, and models were produced for the various trades and professions. In his *Tableau de Paris*, the utopian writer Sébastien Mercier notes a connection between the professions and the wig in which appear kitchen assistants, lawyers, professors, choirmasters, scribes and notaries, plus judges and wigmakers themselves.*

Much the same occurred in England, where the fashion swept through farmlands and was such a runaway success among the working classes that it was soon hard to find anyone with natural hair, unless – as was the case of Samuel Pepys – it was in the form of a periwig that, either from vanity or fear of pestilence, he ordered to be made from his own sacrificed mane.

If it had once belonged in the higher spheres of society, as a kitsch yet revered mark of distinction, by the beginning of the eighteenth century it was a ubiquitous consumer product around which outlandish commercial practices flourished, including the use of young women willing to give up their tresses in exchange for aprons and handkerchiefs (never, according to Villaret, for money), itinerant salesmen offering second-hand items, and even the creation of illegal workshops, which on the margins of establishments with royal approval, offered wigs that had belonged to victims of the guillotine or models made from horsehair or wool that could easily be confused with mops.

In spite of the fact that hair has been associated with power, and among the ancient Gauls its length was like an aura of honour and freedom that never completely faded in the collective imagination, the rapid spread of the wig (it would infest North America as early as 1660) could not only be put down to monetary aspirations or an arriviste quest for status. Conspicuous consumption, which, according to Thorstein Veblen, defines

* A century earlier Jean-Baptiste Thiers published a detailed denouncement of the clergy's uncontrollable penchant for deceitful locks; using an arsenal of flamboyant quotations and references authorized by councils, his *Histoire des peruques* (A History of Wigs, 1690) is a furious compendium of the ecclesiastical misuse of hairpieces.

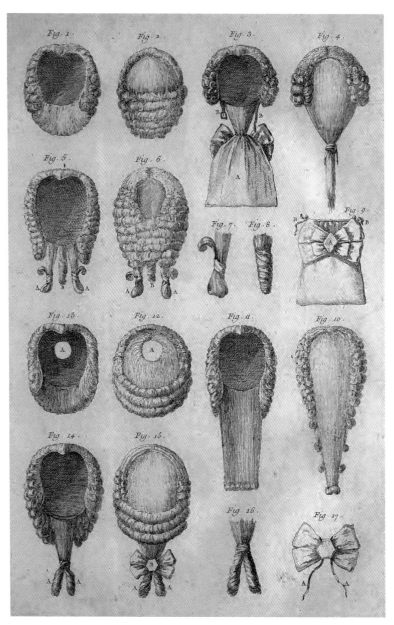

R. Bénard, after J. R. Lucotte, 'Wigs in a Wigmaker-barber Shop',
with figures 12 and 13 depicting tonsured models. Engraving in
D. Diderot and J. le Rond d'Alembert, *Recueil de planches,
sur les sciences et les arts* (1771).

social status and tends to be emulated in a form of struggle for recognition and class privilege, made the wig a ravelled object of desire – especially in an era such as the Baroque, with its devotion to the god of appearance – perhaps to the extent of covering the Western hemisphere in a heavy cloud of hair.*

There is clear evidence, such as that given by Pepys in his *Diary*, indicating that without a good wig, it was impossible to ascend the social ladder or attain a modicum of respectability (although he himself offers other, very good, reasons for their use, among them avoiding the need to wash: 'I did try two or three borders and periwigs, meaning to wear one, and yet I have no stomach for it; but that the pains of keeping my hair clean is so great'); and while in those days a glance at the wig was enough to locate someone in the social hierarchy (those who had no choice but to display their bald eggheads must have lived in poverty), it is hard to believe that such a contagious fever was the result of a simple desire for ownership that we would nowadays describe as 'aspirational'.

Like those sudden explosions of life that mark the fossil record, in just a few years wigmakers produced over a hundred different models, each with its own name; an exuberance, an authentic experimental orgy that makes one think that those shaggy fantasies touched deeper chords and unleashed more primitive impulses than those of ascent and rank. In his 1799 *Éloge des perruques* (In Praise of Wigs), which contains as many panegyrics as passages on history, Dr Akerlio describes

---

* As far as is known, the Versailles fashion for wigs conquered all the courts of Europe, and only the recalcitrant Frederick William I of Prussia preferred to keep to the old military style; he did not, however, prohibit its use among his servants and subjects.

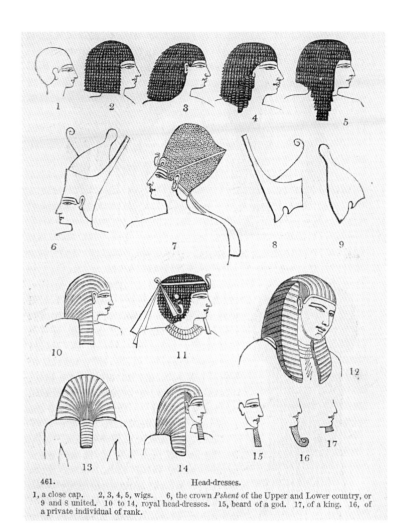

461.   Head-dresses.

1, a close cap.   2, 3, 4, 5, wigs.   6, the crown *Pshent* of the Upper and Lower country, or 9 and 8 united.   10 to 14, royal head-dresses.   15, beard of a god.   17, of a king.   16, of a private individual of rank.

'Crowns and headdresses of the Ancient Egyptians', by J. Gardner Wilkinson, illustrated in *A Popular Account of the Ancient Egyptians* (1854). Figures 2–5 are conventional wigs; 10–14 denote royalty. The beard in figure 15 shows divinity.

a considerable number of models: from the 'Caracalla' to the 'Venus', the 'Spanish', the 'Aspasia' and, finally, the 'Sartine', which caught on in England and would become the emblem of the judiciary.

The oppressive, fickle nature of fashion might explain why a man without financial means arranges his hair so that it looks as if he is wearing a wig. (The sense of confidence conferred by conformity of appearance, the satisfaction of pleasing the social guardian and its many eyes, may be greater, as Oscar Wilde insists, than the call of any religion.) But that simulacrum of a simulacrum, pitiful in its convoluted transparency, counterproductive as a mark of distinction, scarcely compares with those supernatural manes that became obligatory for no apparent reason, and were of a length and thickness that no human head could possibly have sustained: lush, leafy trees made from twenty mops of hair, stunning towers like moose antlers that attract attention and follow the logic of coquettish excess. The rage for wigs may well have had to do with the quest for social status or, as is sometimes insisted, hygiene (in those times, bathing was a sporadic practice and shaven heads prevented the invasion of undesirable fauna), but there is no doubt that the fascination of body enlargement was also involved, the mysterious alchemy between the face and its astonishing frame: the possession of a new, malleable excrescence with a semiotic appendage.

Envy, and the mimetic desire that sustains it – the wish to acquire and possess what others have, the urge to imitate the way others present themselves in public with their new appearance and their ability to squander money, through an authentic pyramid of desire understood as excess rather than lack – had much to do with this process, and Jean Baudrillard, in his *For*

The wig as language, advertisement in a 1964 Frederick's
of Hollywood catalogue.

a Critique of the Political Economy of the Sign, showing himself to be closer to Veblen than Marx, lays stress on the importance of consumer goods, in terms of not only their use or exchange value, but their value as a sign.

Just as with the wristwatch, perfume and other items of personal care, the wig was one of the sumptuary articles that were promoted and then multiplied at the very dawn of capitalism as bearers of prestige, coveted for what they represented in the establishment of taste and style, of a notion of identity with class domination at its root. Beyond the fact that, as classical political economy would have us believe, the wig fulfils certain hygienic functions or the needs of vanity, its unchecked proliferation can be related to its appearance as an authentic language, an elaborated system of signs that, among other things, both disrupted and gave substance to the strata of the social hierarchy.

If in the early eighteenth century no one had any desire to be excluded from the euphoria of acquiring an unforeseen crowning glory, a repertoire of filamentary antennae that, to cap it all, was impregnated with essences and colours, and emitted sexually explicit messages, it should be remembered that those messages were not exclusively related to rank and well-being, but also to excess and diversion, to transgression, display and, of course, shared appetites. Those urbane antlers might have been a guarantee of good taste and status within a social code, but who would have passed up the opportunity to elevate his or her body and, from those heights, broadcast signals to the four corners of the planet? Who would have refused to play the game of adding a touch of illusion and immoderation to the language of physical presence?

Samson at the Roland-Garros

The primitive call of hair, its unbounded fertility, that bristling which pierces and exceeds the sexual, becomes muddled and distorted when the hairpiece comes into play. Is it in fact an equally simulated force? Is some of its power transferred through contact or proximity, as happens with locks of hair in black magic? Or is it that those people who use wigs feel in some way aggrandized due to the impression created by their studied metamorphoses?

Although it is highly questionable whether Samson would have recovered his powers by using a hairpiece or toupee, this would perhaps have intimidated the Philistines and disconcerted the woman who made him lose his head without the use of a blade. When Delilah employed her wiles to carry out the symbolic castration of the man she pretended to love, she could not have been sure that the excrescence which gave him strength wouldn't grow back overnight. Perhaps Samson – like the rebel Aristomenes of Messene, famous for his Spartan resistance, a model of courage and daring – had the 'hairy heart' of a lion (as the poet Vicente Aleixandre terms it) and, despite the prophecy that marked him from birth, his strength in fact sprang from his inner self rather than his hair.

As a form of media-age Samson who had to face the implacable Delilah of alopecia, Andre Agassi was haunted by the fear that his premature hair loss would lead to a decline of his strength on the courts. From childhood, his appearance had been for him a weapon, the seal of his brazen, strident understanding of tennis, only comparable with his astounding ability to return serve. By the age of eighteen, his scalp had become the main rival to be beaten in his determination to emulate the feel of concrete rather than grass, the lunar surfaces of the American Open rather than the green irregularities of Wimbledon. Was it possible for an improbable rock star of a genteel sport, an Axl Rose lost on the ATP circuit who wins out over such well-groomed legends as Jimmy Connors, to turn up with that display of follicular deforestation, a shiny pate only accentuated by flashbulbs and reflectors? Would anyone have the nerve to challenge the venerable tennis institutions with a bank clerk's receding hairline?

Agassi understood that part of his professional role was to play a part, to make the mask of the rebel his own. But how was he to achieve this if one aspect of his identity, a drive based on heterodoxy and scandal, was beginning to appear on his pillow each morning and disappear in swirling eddies down the plughole? It was nature – not Delilah – that was castrating him, imposing an early autumn on his appearance, watering down his image as a sporting pirate. His top spin might be unaffected, but if he had made his entrance on court as a defiant, photogenic Samson in shorts, determined to ruffle a game that was still all too spruce, a conservative sport with a long lineage that at one point in its history was played with balls filled with human hair, then baldness was much more than a mere mishap: it was an undeniable setback.

Defeated by the unbearable burden of hair loss, with some strange form of enthusiasm he resigned himself to wearing a hairpiece. His audacity and lack of inhibition led him to choose a wig: unlike such other bald athletes as the Bulgarian goalkeeper Borislav Mikhailov, who leapt about between the posts with a thick but sober toupee fixed to his scalp with gorilla glue, Agassi opted for a model with highlighted spikes above a long mane, producing the mental image of ferocious power and an exuberance that did not yield easily to the phlegm of tennis, its whiff of the aristocratic. Then, in a supreme feint, he tamed these locks with a headband of electrifying colours that, in fact, held the wig in place more firmly. Although shouts of 'Punk!' were heard from the stands, Agassi, with the disdain of a person who thinks dressing in white has a moral significance, disguised the fact that some part of his offence, half of the dynamite laid at the foundations of tennis, was completely fake and required daily maintenance.

As if he were the victim of the character he had created and the puppet itself were manipulating him with strings as fine as hair that he could not break, the stardom that had raised him to the peak also cast him back into his own trap. In a counter-play of astonishing errors he found himself cornered into proclaiming – without, of course, a hint of confession or irony – that 'Image is everything.' A publicity campaign for Canon cameras had him repeating that compromising slogan, the inverted mantra that would have been hilarious if it were not that it described the tragedy of a man ensnared in his own simulations, condemned to draw strength from falsehoods. Although beneath his outsider appearance there was an equilibrium in his measured, powerful game that accepted the, in this case, unspeakable adjective 'elegant', Agassi still had not won a Grand Slam tournament, was still a promising youngster, a noisy talent who ran the risk of falling off the precipice of bravado, so the predictable slogan that was suddenly ubiquitous, and which spectators returned to him as an insult, appearing in large print with each serious defeat, took on new, increasingly pitiless meanings. Inside the chalk tramlines, in the inverse of sport converted into a branch of show business, that mistaken, opportunistic slogan was read as an increasingly strained version of 'There is nothing but the image.'

In tennis, described by all and sundry as 'the most solitary of sports', concentration and mental control are as important as fitness, and it is easy to imagine the uphill on-court struggle when half of one's brain is focused on ensuring that the wig does not go flying. In Paris, in his first Grand Slam final, just one match away from showing that his look wasn't just a front, a mere empty marketing mask, Agassi was more concerned for the stability of his wig than his opponent's game. The night before the final, in something approaching operatic melodrama, a catastrophe occurred: he had used the wrong conditioner and his wig began to fall apart in his hands. Not even a kilogram of grips could have solved his capillary emergency, so the following day, with a band around his forehead and the wig held together by hairpins, rather than mentally visualizing himself raising the trophy as the newly crowned champion, he again and again envisioned a fateful scene: after a difficult shot, the wig falls to the clay; the centre court of the Roland-Garros stadium morphs into the mouth of an astonished, breathless monster with occasional shouts that seem more like the hair-raising crash of the bottom falling out of reality. A fox? Has someone thrown a fox fur onto the court?

In *Open*, one of the few celebrity autobiographies that does not end up being self-indulgent or bland, as if reliving what only

Andre Agassi at the 1990 French Open final in Paris, with his thoughts divided between the championship and his wig.

happened in his head, Agassi describes the droll, eye-popping scene of his recurrent nightmare: 'I imagine millions of spectators move closer to their TV sets, their eyes widening and, in dozens of dialects and languages, ask how Andre Agassi's hair has fallen from his head.' The Ecuadorian player Andrés Gómez, ten years older than Agassi, but with a thick mane that showed no signs of receding, finally won the championship with an unassailable 6–3, 2–6, 6–4, 6–4.

Years later, redemption would come at Wimbledon, when Agassi, by then proudly bald and dressed in white, was ready for not only victory but marriage to the queen of tennis, Steffi Graf. There is no proof that he was reading Synesius' *In Praise of Baldness*, that philosophical skit on real and false hair, that light-hearted defence of the apparently indefensible: the mass desertion of hair, the incorruptible smoothness of the scalp, the head a third bum cheek – according to Francisco de Quevedo's rather coarse but pleasant simile. But before his life could take a turn and he was able to attain a period of cloying reconciliation worthy of the ending of the sort of cheesy film shown on long coach journeys in Mexico, Agassi, who was obsessed with his image while he was resisting being stereotyped by it, who felt himself to be stripped bare by the fall of what he believed to be his identity, did perhaps, on his own account, achieve the stripped-down wisdom of Eduardo Galeano, that other 'capillary mutant' who, disgusted by the humiliation of barbers charging him half-price, wrote: 'If hair was important, it would be on the inside of the head, not the outside.'

The Counter-philosophy
of the Wig

J ust one step from waste matter, the lowest of the low,
an embodiment of falsehood and vanity, the wig has
never belonged in the sphere of thought. As with clothing and
other trivialities – daily life, for instance – anything branded
as banal is of no concern to the philosopher, or not at least to
the philosopher who develops his ideas in the vast empire of
the footnote on a passage from Plato, the coordinates of which
are fixed by immutability and permanence. An absurdity in
comparison with the problem of Being, contingent and insignificant in the face of need, doubly contemptible for its seductive
dimension and perceptible impurity, hair has no place in the
hierarchy of illustrious topics, and much less the wig, which, as
a simulacrum, fluttering in the wind far removed from the duty
of imitation, would almost seem to flaunt its unreality.

But there was a time when those philosophers intolerant of
all things hirsute, those minds resistant to the smaller things
in life that are contaminated by non-being, sheltered under
exuberant, well-groomed wigs; two long centuries during which
the elevated discourse of philosophy, staunch expurgator of the
trivial, found the ritual of donning another's hair essential. Why
did none of those male philosophers give a second thought to
the perturbing organic mass that crowned their heads each
morning? Had the infamy of existence and the degradation

of the ordinary reached such extremes as to leave no room for questions about that hairy architecture, about that mammalian headwear that gazed back at them from the mirror on a daily basis?

If a meeting of philosophers had been organized in classical antiquity, the most celebrated of them – beginning with Socrates and Diogenes – would have proudly exhibited a smooth forehead, brilliant in every sense of the word. Despite the fact that Plato was only able to display a latent receding hairline, and that Aristotle, Epicurus, Heraclitus and Parmenides all had quite flourishing tresses, in the archetypal image the Greek thinker is bald as a coot with a thick compensatory beard, but devoid of the impetuosity of youth. That is the picture that Synesius, 'the most valiant of bald men', records and transmits in his *In Praise of Baldness,* in part to do justice to his own devastated scalp, but also to stress that hair – that animal accident, that unpredictable, superfluous attribute – has nothing in common with the heights of abstraction. If his humorous text is to be believed, the majority of classical philosophers lived in that state of asymmetry, that tension between 'barren pate' and 'populated understanding'.*

But if a collection of the busts of Greek philosophers could be mistaken for a museum of androgenic alopecia in which the marble itself contributes to the mirage of a melancholy

---

* That somewhat superstitious association between baldness and wisdom was still alive in the early nineteenth century. In *Art coiffer soi-même* (The Art of Hairstyling for Women), M. Villaret writes: 'Nothing is more common than hairpieces since the seat of intellectual power is in a constant state of ardour, with the consequence, in the majority of cases, of premature loss of hair from the upper part of the head where the ferment is at work.'

exhibition of full moons, in the modern era – less given to statuary – an assembly of that nature would include samples of
wigs. Descartes, Locke, Leibniz, Berkeley, Rousseau, Hume,
Kant . . . all have a place reserved in the grand album of the
hairpiece, and although the philosopher himself might brand it
as frivolous, strictly excluded from higher authority, it is worth
considering the consequences of the fact that modern philosophy,
incapable of applying Occam's razor to its own excrescences, to
its unquestioned habits, achieves its fulfilment in the shelter of
some form of hairy bonnet.

Descartes, who thought wigs were beneficial to health, had
at least four in the colour of his actual hair; it is uncertain if
this was because they allowed him to pass unnoticed and so
continue the unsociable and solitary lifestyle he preferred, or if
he collected them because they were formidable confirmation
that everything related to the body and appearance is volatile,
secondary, non-essential.* Kant's wig, in contrast, was white,
stiffer and more codified, and while, to judge by James Boswell's
description of their meeting, it was so ill-fitting that his servant was constantly employed in straightening it, he was never
without it, as if the hairpiece were the literal condition of the

---

* The ruse of wearing a black model, identical to his own hair, possibly
contributed to the legend that, in a century dedicated to the wig,
Descartes flatly refused to don one and preferred to wear his natural hair
long. However, he in fact adopted the practice shortly after turning forty
to hide his greying locks, although he was later careful to ask Claude
Picot, his right-hand man in Paris, to order them with a few grey hairs
so that they looked more convincing. While he extolled their protective
virtues, they were of little use to him during the impossible Stockholm
mornings when he had to get up before dawn to instruct Queen
Christina of Sweden in a freezing master class that would eventually cost
him his life. (Queen Christina had an equal penchant for masculine wigs
and, in Paris, enjoyed living as a man.)

Workshop of Klose and Wollmerstädt, *Kant and Friends at the Table*, 1892–3, coloured wood engraving after the Emil Doerstling Rococo painting, which could also be called *After-dinner Wigged Conversation*.

possibility of his experience, the necessary frame – a sort of hirsute a priori – of his public and professional lives.

In the seventeenth and eighteenth centuries, the use of the wig was so widespread that not even such an enemy of super-fluous adornment as Jean-Jacques Rousseau would have had the courage to spurn it. Having resolved to restrict himself to a diet of independence and austerity that eschewed any form of sophistication and luxury, rather than wholly dispense with his wig, the defender of the noble savage and the return to nature exchanged it for a simpler model. Was it still a mark of distinction even for those who constantly insisted on the equality of all men? Was the hairpiece, perched upon the social body, so ubiquitous that it became invisible, even to the cham-pions of *sapere aude*, the proponents of independent thought and Enlightenment? Could it be that the very genealogy of importance they contributed to tracing – that definition of what could be considered to fall within the realm of philosophy, that reality stratified by rank – made them incapable of reflecting on that age-old custom, so it never even crossed their minds that the wig was in fact a figure of ostentation and excess, pomp and appearance, the outrageous trophy of its visibility? Could it be that the wig in some way thought in them – *through* them – like a reflection of that unnoticed but standardizing and disciplinary weight with which society and its symbolic practices structure and give form not only to thought but to the body?

Such questions were never even posed. The philosophers might groom their wigs each night and ensure that they were made by the best coiffeurs in Paris, but although they were only separated by the thin wall of the cranium, thought and the wig never met. With the possible exception of Leibniz, who, in the spirit of the Baroque, elaborated a philosophy of facade and, by extension, of the wig (of the need for a division between independent, monadic thought and that other sphere which offers itself to society and deals with its conventions and obligations), their concerns moved in the opposite direction from what was nesting on their heads. If philosophy could no longer turn its back on the world of appearance without suffering the consequences, it did not seem prepared for the scandal of the simulacrum, that discordant third party that does not aspire to being a copy of anything, that subverts the opposition between the model and the copy, and, with the bare-faced cheek of its artifice, simply intends to produce an effect.

With their attachment to the trifling, those who address such superfluous issues as hair do not belong in the lineage of philosophy – although they perhaps find a place in literature or

The skull of Gottfried Wilhelm von Leibniz projected onto a portrait engraving in which he is wearing his baroque wig, published in *Zeitschrift für Ethnologie* by W. Krause (15 November 1902) as 'proof' of the authenticity of Leibniz's remains.

open provocation. The mere questioning of which themes merit elucidation is an act of dissidence, a step outside hegemonic tradition; due to the non-conformity of the gesture, the eccentricity of the quest, the person who does question must be willing to bear disdainful references: a juggler of insignificant trifles, a hunter of trivialities, a clown of thought. After adding a touch of humour and irreverence to Platonic dialogue (to stop it walking on air, as he explained), Lucian of Samosata, author of *The Fly, an Appreciation,* was accused of philosophical high treason, while Dion of Prusa, who wrote *Encomium on Hair,* was, after Philostratus, pigeonholed as some form of sophist since it is in the manner of sophists 'to take these matters seriously' (and it goes without saying that a philosopher has no business amusing himself with a paradoxical encomium, with the exaltation of what is low and paltry or with problems that no one would dream of sculpting in philosophical marble). Not to mention Michel de Montaigne's officious expulsion from philosophy and his displacement into literature for having dared to 'reflect so brilliantly on such insignificant topics' as thumbs, wearing clothes, smells and idleness.

Amusement, fun, essays. Margins in which peck exiles from that centre philosophy recognizes as its own under the dictum of 'the real is rational and rational is real.' If, after Plato, one of the tasks of philosophy had consisted of producing difference – distinguishing between the authentic and the spurious – who was going to say that right there, on the very heads of its apostles, it was necessary to set an untimely bird of ill omen that eludes the contrast between essence and appearance, the scandal of the simulacrum, the wig that no longer aspires to resemble anything 'original', that claims possession of its own imposture, its clearly false truth and, in the triumph of its lack of resemblance, its phantasmal apotheosis beyond life and death, evades the degradation of being a mere copy of a copy?

Nothing but a sophist head of hair. Hair with no other grounding principle than the impression it makes. Without roots but flaunting its foliage. Mask hair. And where else but on the crowns of the most distinguished philosophers?

The Future Was a Purple Wig

The future continues to age. Of all its characteristics, the most endearing may be that we have already seen it go by and it looks as old-fashioned and remote as the past itself. Once 1984 had been put behind us with perplexing ease, with not a sign of the mental tyranny imagined by George Orwell; once the distant 2001 had come to a close without the unsettling endowment of emotional machines (even during that year marked in red, swollen and deformed by the weight of apprehension, it was thought that 2001 was nothing more than a mirage created by distance), we were trapped in the paradox of science fiction, in that involuntary loop, as unprecedented as a time machine, in which it seems that the best way to visit the future is by immersion in nostalgia.

After the Second World War, and shortly before *Star Wars* (a movie set 'a long time ago'), films and television series projected the image of an ingenuous, obsolete future, where speed and exploration of the atom sink their roots into a clearly geriatric passion. Even the menace of the *other* – of an interplanetary encounter and possible extermination – is tinged with improbably bright and receptive hues, as if, although under threat, the joy of knowing that we are not alone in the universe comes to the fore.

Whether it is because their spaceships are packed with tubing and their asteroids still made of papier-mâché or polystyrene, the old representation of what is to come has something intangibly innocent about it, something of a motley crew of clowns or a cosmic masked ball, typical of a period in which tomorrow still does not exist. However rudimentary it may seem nowadays, the imagination was at that time conjugated in the present perfect; there was an urgent need to flee as quickly as possible from the tense, icy post-war environment in which mushroom clouds emerged on the horizon.

With black and white having given way to full Technicolor, many large- and small-screen productions predicted a universe in which women took leading roles. From the deliriously psychotronic *El planeta de los mujeres invasores* (Planet of the Female Invaders, 1966) to the more sombre UFO television series, with its operating-theatre conception of flying saucers, passing through *Barbarella*, that visionary peephole in which Jane Fonda plays a galactic Venus, the universe is full of metallic women, endowed with a beauty that would have met Rubens's approval, who set out to conquer space in skintight, translucent jumpsuits or vaporous uniforms. (Maybe because they are more appropriate for the starry night of the cosmos, there are spacesuits that come perilously close to being negligees.)

As a contemporary mirror offering a glimpse of the good things to come, a sidereal extrapolation for the reinvention of the image those times had formed of themselves, B-movies and -series entrusted the action to attractive female commanders or voluptuous invaders – all-too-carnal versions of the Future Eve of *Metropolis* – possibly so that the face of the future doesn't gaze back at us, or at least not too soon, with its expression of vexation and disillusion.

In that behind-the-times but topical vision bordering on anime, the costumes take their inspiration from the most surprising eras; as with any monster worth its salt, the future is composed of parts from anywhere and everywhere. In a somewhat military environment, more appropriate to time-warped centurions than astronauts, plastic and spurious metals dominate, and even long-past elements are redeemed by a synthetic facelift. An age-old accessory like the wig, which takes the love of ringlets to baroque extremes, returns as a helmet, partly aerodynamic, partly *à gogo*, in order to highlight the qualities of straightness and electrifying dyes. The intergalactic purple of the hairstyles on UFO's lunar base represents, without any other assistance – as did Yves Klein's international blue – a whole era, in this case those two or three nostalgic decades in which something was still expected of the future.

As dowdy clothing would have clashed with the notion of space exploration, future fashion is chic and body-hugging, a far cry from the unattractive white sleeping bags worn by visitors to the International Space Station. Although the fabrics tend to be rather antiseptic and robotically cold, curvaceous lines are still in abundance; the triumph of technology appears to keep salaciousness at bay but, by using perfect bodies and radioactive wigs akin to something produced by genetic engineering or a dream formula, human sexuality somehow holds its own during routine voyages into hyperspace – although the replicant touch is never completely refuted. The truth is that close encounters of the third kind open a door to erotic fantasies. What is abduction but an intimate kidnapping involving an interplanetary mixing of DNA?

In Mexico, wrestlers frequently used to appear in science-fiction films. When El Santo and Blue Demon tired of merely

Jane Fonda in *Barbarella* (1968), directed by Roger Vadim.

flying through the air in the ring, they extended their battle against evil to attacks from other galaxies. Although the idea of extraterrestrials playing tag teams and skilfully applying back-breakers is hilarious, the conjunction of masks and wigs that the subgenre of *lucha libre* involves is not so completely different from the worlds it sets spinning: if the outlandish hairstyles and pointy helmets of science fiction shoot us far away from the present and its unmistakably earthbound habits, in *lucha libre* the most famous, most emblematic dispute is the confrontation of the mask and hair. In the extended knot of a lock, while the two bodies are at maximum tension, as if testing the truth of their muscles, everything is suddenly reduced to a battle for identity. The rival might well be a camouflaged extraterrestrial, an invader or a replicant with a human mask, so it is never a bad idea to threaten the disguise with exposure, or at least diminish its power by the old trick of snatching it off.

From then on, after that slightly astonishing conjecture – which, for a retrospective, the Mexican curator Itala Schmelz rightly termed 'the nearer future' – the future gradually faded until it almost vanished. And if nowadays its fantasy barely reaches to the next weekend, what is to be done with those huge plans to colonize the moon, with the whole iconography of rockets and modular rooms, of android translators and artificial planets where Martians and humans will finally meet?

Reduced to a vintage album, the future has ceased to be a capsule hanging many light years away in space, from which the darkness of the present can be viewed. Rather than being

Hair turns purple on the lunar base. Antonia Ellis in the role of Lieutenant Joan Harrington in the TV series UFO (1970–73), created by Gerry and Sylvia Anderson with Reg Hill.

relaunched into the stratosphere as the ultimate objective of thought, the future has been relegated to something less than a game: a mere outlandish souvenir. There is hardly a fancy-dress shop in existence that does not have a space amazon costume, metallic cape and electric wig included, displayed beside a Dracula, a Cleopatra or an elusive Casanova. But then, the fancy-dress shop is just a nuanced rubbish bin of the imagination.

As the future debacle goes on, as perspective art continues to increase its dioptres and progress is enlisted as just another superstition, what is left for us but to treasure that whimsical, slightly faded but still daring instant in which the future donned a purple wig?

The Mannequin and
the Dark Object of Desire

Their cold white bodies can be glimpsed during seasonal changeovers, in the windows of shops that have fallen on hard times, possibly on the shoulders of a dealer hesitating to clutch the crotch. This is also when they display their baldness. Although Giorgio de Chirico used to paint them with smooth heads lacking features or hair, geometric and provocative in their wooden sleekness, mannequins generally wear wigs. Of course there are models – particularly the male varieties – whose hair is little more than a dense mass of fibreglass, and some are dispatched headless from the factory; but beheading as a form of economy or follicular mimesis devoid of detail not only reduces the sex appeal but even destroys the notion of the showcase as a small theatre frozen in time.

As the elder sister of the china doll, a finished, voluptuous version of the tailor's dummy, the mannequin is a clothes hanger that, owing to its aloof attractiveness, because it embodies a fleeting illusion of beauty (our notion of the *ideal* changes so rapidly that the life expectancy of a mannequin is only seven years) will be forever wedded to merchandise, to the ultimately venal offering, often to be seen only a few steps away from the prostitutes who – no less absent and magnetic, the two standing in identical poses, with that stillness about to be belied by what particularly inhabits the realm of the mind – await their clients, exposed to another form of desire.

The fragility of the mannequin is more evocative of the human body than a statue. Once made of wax or papier-mâché, they quickly either melted under the spotlights or languidly shed their outer layers like a bud eaten by the void. As a result of humidity and floods, many of them ended their days as muddy masses of paper and paste, proof of their distant kinship with the Golem. Nowadays when they get chipped or cracked, their exposed areas are something akin to dry wounds, scars that have never bled, or even, when the cracks are so fine they are hardly visible, like wrinkles or photogenic veins. Eternally young, with lips painted bright crimson, suspended in an unalterable present, reminiscent of metaphysical art, there are still mannequins whose shabbiness and dusty surfaces seem less the product of neglect or natural deterioration than of premature old age, of the unimaginable vice and corruption of matter.

It is not only the most expensive and realistic models, with their additions of false teeth and glass eyes, that use natural hair. Apart from the mannequins of wig-sellers (almost always busts with no other clothing than a scarf or a kerchief), the principal decoration of a mannequin is the stunning silkiness of its hair. When this is not synthetic, it is the only organic element of a simulacrum in which organic shapes and curves are reproduced on a scale of one-to-one; the spectacular scene of a body that is inert, yet also full of life, benefiting from the effect of abstract sensuality.

Skin made up in vaguely credible shades, encrusted false nails, long, black eyelashes heavy with mascara, flowing locks that, however, appear quite stiff, stockings and suspender belts

Abandoned
mannequin
in an old wig
shop, 2012.

that are not removed for weeks at a time: all are factors that
distance the mannequin from the sculptural arts, and transport
it, as a foreign body, to the realm of taxidermy, where the repet-
itive act of dressing and undressing it reveals that the fabric
corresponds to its real skin. In more prudish times, the seasonal
rite of changing costume would have caused a commotion if
undertaken in broad daylight; it wasn't just to create a sense of
surprise that shop windows were covered and screens placed
around the mannequins: one store was censured for daring to
display corsets on a model called Miss Modesty, in spite of the
fact that, as if in a reflex action – a friendly wink on the part of
the designer – the mannequin with the breathtaking waistline
was covering her face with her hands.

In a fascinating photograph, *Maniquí tapado* (Covered Mannequin), taken in 1931, the Mexican photographer Manuel Álvarez Bravo captures the prudery and eroticism aroused by the sight of a half-dressed mannequin; her permanent smile takes on a double meaning in conjunction with stockings rolled at the knees (an effect that Marcel Duchamp would later utilize in the Gotham Book Mart as a window display for André Breton's *Arcanum 17*, in which a scantily clad, headless mannequin stands in magical, dreamlike lighting in the paradoxical pose of someone reading a book). It is hardly surprising that, particularly when abandoned to their fate or only half-dressed, mannequins have been a recurrent theme in photography. The works of Cartier-Bresson, José Alemany, John Claridge, Elliott Erwitt and Arthur Fellig (Weegee) offer numerous examples of the love affair between the frozen image and these docile models, who have the indisputable advantage of not even so much as breathing.

Rather than being set on a prestigious pedestal, mannequins are often maintained upright by a rod, a very long spinal column that runs through their bodies, anchoring them to the floor, and which acts as much as a crutch as a stake (the effects of this eternal torture sometimes cause their parted lips to seem even more unsettling and pleading). The chrome rod, which introduces an orthopaedic element, reveals the instability of the mannequin and, simultaneously, its proximity to the prosthesis: as a mechanism for attracting the gaze, the mannequin cannot replace any organ or limb, but it stands in for the body we will never have. Although the Dutch word *manneken* originally referred to a 'small man' (figurine), it became a life-size clothes hanger on which to drape our longings or idealized self-images.

Wooden torsos dating from ancient Egypt, faithful replicas of pharaohs, are still in existence. In Rome, certain empresses had detailed copies of themselves made to assist in their choice of clothing – and possibly also as a rest for a particularly sumptuous wig while it was being restyled, while in his *Natural*

Weegee (Arthur H. Fellig), *Mannequins*, 1942, photograph.

History Pliny mentions the existence of glass mirrors lined with gold leaf. The mannequin, however, for those who could afford the luxury, was valued more highly than that luxurious item, a replacement for obsidian, bronze or the calm of water: the reflection offered by the doll, in addition to being palpable and scenic, could be walked around, and was always flattering.

Since it refers to the passive body in the act of offering itself up, but also the corpse, since it slides a disconcerting wedge between reality and representation, the mannequin is closely related to the concept of the double. In Rodolfo Usigli's novel *Ensayo de un crimen* (Rehearsal for a Crime), which was adapted for the screen by Luis Buñuel in 1955, a model who poses for the manufacture of mannequins thinks of them as bloodless relatives, her paralysed twins. In a plotline involving a lover, a sexualized doll and mortal remains, she exchanges her clothes for the mannequin's, knowing that even the underwear will be a perfect fit. This action leads to another, more decisive change: by a stroke of luck, the woman, played by the actress Miroslava in the film, manages to save her skin at the last moment and the mannequin ('a disquieting muse', according to de Chirico), who is dragged by the hair in a scene that is at once surrealistic and cavemanesque (the leg left lying on the floor for a few seconds is unforgettable), replaces her in what can only be classified as a parody of murder.

In *Eroticism*, originally published in 1957, Georges Bataille argues that the more unreal a woman's form – the further it is from her natural weight and true physiology – the greater the erotic potential. Mannequins, freed from the hirsute animal state, from that pelt with its hint of the anthropoid, but also with no need to make physical use of their limbs – their function being limited to the service of beauty – embody the most widespread image of the desirable woman. But just as unreal, hairless and even fragile female forms prefigure or promise other, more dominant, hairy forms – those sought out by instinct – the mannequin cannot completely dispense with the exaltation of overtly animal parts. In order to arouse temptation, to avoid being mistaken for bland clothes hangers and so fulfil their real function as irresistible perches for consumption, mannequins heed the hypnotic, salacious call of the wig.

Andy Warhol's Wig

In the summer of 2006, in the New York offices of Christie's, Andy Warhol's wig sold for $10,800, almost double the expected price. The bundle of platinum-blond hair, cut pageboy style, that the artist began to wear in the late 1950s achieved, for the second time, its predictable fifteen minutes of fame after offering constant and not the least discreet service to an owner who had converted it into the centrepiece of his image, elevated to the state of a consumer product. The auctioned wig was not, of course, the only one in his wardrobe (his penchant for duplication, for copies of the copy, led him to amass more than thirty spiky hairpieces, not to mention those worn by his double), and was far from being the first: that particular specimen dated back to the 1980s, when, blurring the boundaries between art and frivolity, narcissism and self-promotion, Warhol no longer appeared in public without his filamentary finery, the pop headdress that identified him as an art superstar.

Exhibited for sale on a mannequin, without the sunglasses and the face with the rough-hewn but delicate features that gave it bulk, that wig (indistinguishable from its clones, precisely because it is one among many others, because it participates in the drive for repetition) has a peculiar, almost dreamlike aura from being so frequently seen, so enigmatic despite the repetition, that distances it from the status of a mere hairpiece, and makes it lean towards the fetish, as a metallic crest for which imposture and artificiality have become second nature.

Andy Warhol began to lose his hair at an early age. The impassive factory of his follicles refused to undertake the serial production of filaments for which it had been intended, and although the budding artist had already demonstrated a level of dissatisfaction with his physical appearance, the exterminating angel of baldness reaffirmed his determination to take control of his identity as a quick-change artist.

After exhibiting the painting *The Broad Gave Me My Face, But I Can Pick My Own Nose* (1949) in a small gallery, the then Andrew Warhola utilized a great part of his talent for graphic art and store-window design to reconstruct himself, modelling his appearance to suit his own specifications. And thus began an aesthetic but also commercial quest in which cosmetic surgery and capillary scams would play a leading role, one that would end in the definitive supremacy of appearance over being, of glamour over genius, of the recycling of images over a possibly already devalued notion of originality.

As with the mole on Marilyn Monroe's cheek or Elvis Presley's quiff, Warhol's wig is an indisputable seal of United States culture, a permanent nod to irreverence, simulation and parody. Despite the fact that baldness is generally associated with conservatism and comfort, something more likely to apply to a bank manager than an avant-garde artist, in Warhol the early use of a wig achieved the heights of sheer performance: it reaffirmed in appearance terms an aesthetic programme characterized by the appropriation of the lowbrow and the daring deployment of cliché.

Warhol didn't use a wig – that distant token of respectability and power, that former mark of nobility – to crown his unquestionable ascent to the summit of the Fine Arts; nor did he employ it, following the accepted pattern, to hide his baldness or presumed ugliness: he wore a falsely greying, messy, cheap wig to create the unclassifiable, ill-groomed effigy of the scarecrow, of the artist who, through a gesture of self-ridicule and reconstruction, of audacious exhibitionism that, nevertheless, acts as a form of concealment, has made himself into the caricature of a star, an unmistakable, kitsch myth, a symbol of merchandizing.

Warhol's wig is somewhat reminiscent of the dandy, has something of that 'last gleam of the heroic' that Baudelaire insists on so strongly. Once the work and the person are indistinguishable in terms of artistic enunciation, and every step that the author-character does or does not take has been planned with metaphysical attention and re-echoes as an aesthetic act, a sort of parabola laden with double and triple meanings, the act of wearing a wig every day becomes equivalent to issuing a manifesto and eludes (or turns on its head) its affiliation to decadence when it is worn unashamedly, with a brashness that is calculated and ultimately outrageous. Just like Baudelaire, who for a while sported a mythical sky-blue wig, he boasted of its loudness, and like Marcel Duchamp's enigmatic alter ego Rrose Sélavy, who allowed him to carry duplicity beyond the sphere of words, Warhol's decision may have involved a level of buffoonery, but it also constituted a step beyond camouflage, a memorable affront aimed at standing out – rather than merging into the surroundings – which, in its flagrant emphasis on falseness, its refusal to hide the imposture, privileges the hypertelic, distinctiveness or

Andy Warhol in an advertisement for Vidal Sassoon's 'Natural Control' hairspray for men, 1985.

strangeness above all else; the opposite of invisibility. Dandyism as a route for making difference a source of strength.

As an artist with one foot in popular taste, whose referents (principally consumer products, whether they be soup cans or prefabricated gossip-column stars) he never tired of justifying, but with the other in New York high society (Culture with a capital C, with all its rewards of glory, exclusivity and fortune), for Warhol the wig was also a personal support that could no longer be classified as artificial since it allowed him to move from one environment to the other while retaining dissonance in both, to be the man who, through his ironical pose,

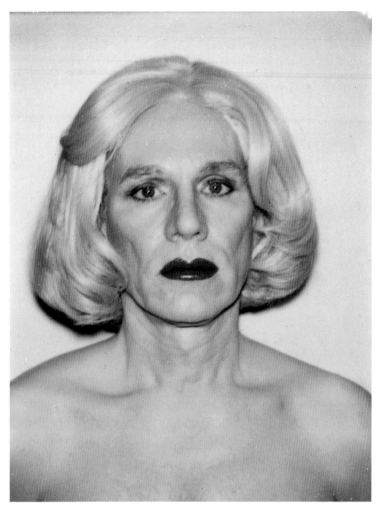

Andy Warhol, *Self-portrait in Drag* (*Monroe Wig*), 1981, Polaroid.

the refractory iciness of his detachment and impassibility, never completely fitted in.

As an irreplaceable piece of his dress-art, Warhol never hoped that his wig would pass unnoticed, but it ended by being such a natural aspect of his plastic image that the synthetic gave the impression of being something that had sprouted from his scalp. So perfect was the coupling of the replica and what it stood in for in his indecisive appearance and latex complexion that, if he had gone to a wig party, in order to meet expectations Warhol would have had to substitute the stylized drag queen models in which he was often photographed for the paradoxical, impersonal disguise of showing himself as he was (at least at the moment of waking): exhibiting his receding hairline, the impressive, unstoppable deforestation of his cranium.

In an era when the wig had lost almost all its ritual connotations, leaving it only as an item of clothing associated with simulation and elusiveness, Warhol shook off its coating of powder to make himself into an unclassifiable piece of merchandise; to play – with every ounce of provocation the situation demanded – the game of consumption without coming out of it too badly damaged. Conscious that he would sooner or later be dragged in by the cog-wheels of fame, to whose perfection he contributed so greatly, keen on the idea of his image being sold prêt-à-porter in fancy-dress shops, even as a mistaken Action Man to partner Barbie, the person who had once answered to the name of Andrew Warhola opted for covering himself in a tangle of platinum blond hair that, while facilitating his elevation to icon, retained the complexity of a lure, a portable art installation.

A machine artist who never renounced his origins as a window dresser, boss of a factory of art-workers on an assembly line, a scrupulous portrayer of himself, Warhol counted on the ploy that his own face would eventually adopt the form of the mask, that the constructed identity and the commercial brand would, in the end, fuse.

The Hemisphere in a Wig

Of all the different parts of the body, there is only one that can be said to stand alone as a constellation. The age-old game of joining the dots in the firmament can result in a sketch of just about any figure, to the extent that constellations of the nose or breasts would not be inconceivable, or even difficult to find. But if postulating such constellations involves a form of mutilation – the shadow of the fetish projected onto the night sky – the same cannot be said of a head of hair, which has a life of its own when detached from the body and can be seen shining in the northern hemisphere under the name of Coma Berenices (Berenice's Hair), beside Boötes (The Herdsman) and below Canes Venatici (The Hunting Dogs of Boötes).

The Greek poet Callimachus was daring enough to write verses on that space-hair from the perspective of that mane itself. The Prosopopoeia, known only in fragments and through Catullus' version – which adds a moral slant – offers the lamentations of a mass of female hair offered up to Aphrodite for the safe return of a husband. What at first sight seems to be a simple rhetorical exercise, an elegiac display spoken by improbably blond booty, becomes a song of separation, a long-distance love poem, thanks to the fact that the hair in question is a cosmos where pain and loss are reflected, and in whose tresses Eros, as ever, becomes entangled.

This head of hair was offered as a sacrifice by Berenice, Queen of Egypt, when her husband, Ptolemy III, returned from a campaign in Assyria. The following day, however, it was stolen from the temple under mysterious circumstances, only to reappear in a more appropriate setting: the sky, where the mathematician Conon of Samos discovered it. Yet there among the ancient stars, the hair continued to suffer. The embodiment of loss, a mesh of aching light, if it once cried for the absence of a loved one, it now whimpered for being so far from the head that was the basis of its attraction.

Hyginus, in his *Poeticon Astronomicon*, records this astonishing story and hints at Conon's opportunism in gaining Ptolemy's favour. The coincidence between the disappearance of the votive hair and the astronomical discovery has led to the conjecture that the furtive Aphrodite had been meddling in the affair from the first: in contrast to Catullus (poem 67), who makes the celestial hair an example of chastity, in Hyginus' version Berenice is thought to have taken advantage of her husband's inroads into foreign territory to have a clandestine affair with Conon, who was then responsible for the robbery. In a twofold act of veneration, as audacious as it was wise, in addition to retaining the capillary keepsake, the lover projected it into the heavens so that, once christened with the name of his impossible love, it would act as a guide through the dark nights of despair.

If the cosmetic is a cosmos, a sphere of order and beauty, hair is the bridge that connects it to external space. Not only the group of stars that cry in the heavens and may have once consoled a man, but the trails of gas and dust left by comets have been represented as errant tresses. With their origins in the Greek *komētēs* (long-haired), comets were conceived as fallen stars, restless planets or ominous atmospheric phenomena. In the final lines of his ode to the constellation of hair, Catullus invokes the downfall of the stars: only in that way will the 'hair-lock' return to Earth with its splendorous trail. Its grief is so profound that the tangle of light even laments the regularity of the cosmos; it knows that only an astral catastrophe capable of transforming the stars into a chaotic mass of damp hair, a confusion of celestial tails that wander headless, would bring about its descent and so reunite it with the queen.

The hair suffers due to its detachability – the above-mentioned sacrificial offering – without being aware that it is only then that it merges into the universe. Baudelaire knew how

The constellation of Coma Berenices (Berenice's Hair), detail of astronomical chart by Sidney Hall, 1825.

to navigate and lose himself in one of those blue-black heads of hair that, with the opium of their aroma, transported him to the past, to his surprising days as a mariner, when he unwillingly voyaged towards the edge of the northern hemisphere, to Calcutta, with the slowness and anxiety of someone who hopes to be washed up on the island of a woman's ear.

At once a coffer and an ocean, a treasure and an abyss, the head of hair that intoxicates the poet is a reservoir of memories and an ecstatic form of travel. Although his poetry and prose possibly have their origins in the hair of the Haitian-born Jeanne Duval – his strange deity, his black, nocturnal Venus – they make no mention of the woman as a whole, and even ignore the existence of the rest of her body. Carried away by that dark Niagara, in his noisy style ('If you knew all I see, inhale, listen to in your hair!'), nothing else is capable of interesting him beyond those rebellious, mesmeric, flowing locks that, while leaving him in transports of delight, promise nothing, as infinity promises nothing.

Portraits of Jeanne Duval's black hair, whether written or painted in oils, give a glimpse of a superabundant, curly mane, divine and animal, that, tied back at the nape of her neck in a heavy, poorly formed knot, allows furious strands to escape like the hatching of serpents. The head of hair of a southern Medusa, indomitable and with a life of its own, her tresses dance and bewitch, bite and inject their venom into the traveller who has dared to navigate them and does not know if he can or even wants to turn back.

It is worth considering here what would happen if, for dramatic effect, we were to discover that the vast head of hair was not part of a woman, but in fact a wig, perhaps manufactured from the remains of an inverted offering, from vows to licentiousness and voluptuousness. Maybe the poems would gain in strength and *bizarrerie*, but they would carry to extremes the enchantment of something that merges with constellations or the ocean.

I like to imagine that it was just after reading Baudelaire's poems that Guy de Maupassant found the key to that darkly impressive story 'A Tress of Hair', in which a long lock of almost-red hair, cut from an unknown head, grows in the mind of a wretched man until it reaches the maddening size of the universe.

On the Other Side
of the Mirror of Horror

In the deformation of the body, in its mutilation or mal-function, beats the possibility of a shudder. It is hard to imagine any civilization that has not wished to see itself in the mirror of the other – the deflected or incomplete reflection of itself – or that has not experienced the fascination of the body of the ghoul: that tense, evasive body marked by difference and exclusion that produces and is the incarnation of our deepest fears. (The word 'horror' itself refers to both a monster and the aversion it produces, the awful body and its rejection.)

As if the whole constellation of difference were not enough, or as if to battle with the otherness of the body would entail a leap to representation – the effort to assimilate in symbols – every era has its legion of monsters, every era distorts its own favour-able self-image, and confronts itself with that fearful vision. It is possible that an era would not completely recognize itself unless seen against a sombre, unsettling backdrop; a gallery of uncon-nected, defective, perturbingly similar figures that are not the result of imperfections in the quicksilver but of the urgent need to gaze on our weaknesses and shiver.

Hair, which returns humans to their recondite animality, which confronts them with their own exuberance and wayward-ness, grows in the nocturnal imagination, however hard we try to restrain it with a knife or scissors. From Medusa to the werewolf, from the bearded lady to Mr Hyde, hair is a supplier of shudders, whether because like a nest of vipers it causes paralysis or reveals dormant impulses (follicles, after all, are by nature chinks, conduits to the external world).

Enduring, in a plant-like mode, a living entity that appears to be undaunted by death, hair is related to the border zones of the human, those estranged but neighbouring realms of nature – the vegetal, the animal, the simply organic – which we employ in the creation of the discordant jumble that is the monster.

The relationship between hair and horror is so close, so spontaneous, that the latter word itself derives from the bristling of hair. In Latin, *horreo* refers to the epidermal response to pain or fear (literally, hair standing on end); a response that, when too brusque, even tends to redundancy: to describe something as hair-raising simply repeats the hirsute etymology of the phenomenon. The fact that when faced with the atavistic fear of anything involving hair – that hirsute beast we still are – an electrical impulse alerts our follicles to the danger is just a

The wig that forms part of Norman Bates's murderous metamorphosis in *Psycho* (1960), directed by Alfred Hitchcock.

ghoulish play of mirrors. Like guts that churn at the sight of an explosion of viscera or the eyes that lock onto the fixed, empty gaze of other eyes, an indefinite, clearly mammalian mesh – the ownerless wig, for example – is enough to activate the erector muscle of the hair and produce the horrified response.

One of the components of the fear, the repulsiveness of a mop of hair, is that when detached and converted into a pelt, shorn or reduced to a souvenir, it gives the impression of being about to draw breath. In Rubens's famous painting, the hair of the decapitated Medusa slithers away like serpents, eels and tarantulas. Hair seems more silken and glossy when it crowns the rigour and decomposition of a corpse, and it is no coincidence that in Lemery's 1698 *Dictionaire, ou traité universel des drogues simples* (Dictionary; or, Universal Treatise on Simple Drugs) hair is defined as: 'A species of plant that grows on the head of man, and also in other places.' In his dark, modernist poetry, Efrén Rebolledo envisioned hair as a 'shadowy raven' perched on top of a woman's head, and to allude to the high-contrast triangular smudge of a lover's pubic hair he rummaged around in his nightmares to find the audaciously morbid image of a 'funereal bat with its wings extended'.

The sinister nature of the wig has been amply explored in cinema (think, for example, of Norman Bates's transformation into a parody of his dead mother in Hitchcock's *Psycho*, or the elevator scene in Brian De Palma's *Dressed to Kill*, that formalist thriller, a breathtaking comedy of suspense in which the mere presence of a person wearing a blond wig and dark glasses opens the door to everything ominous), but there is a short, almost unknown novel in which horror literally takes flight thanks to a wig in the process of transformation into menace. *The Flying*

Wig, by Theodore Frederick Poulson, an oddity published in Hawaii in 1948, is a tortuous, shadowy miniature, a musical box of murmurs and suffering, which succeeds in raising the rather domestic horror of female alopecia to the heights of the uncanny, that supernatural horror where hallucination and madness seem to displace the appearance of the ghost.

As with the majority of fantastic literature, Poulson's novella passes from normality to vertigo, from calm to the insinuation of evil. But here, everyday life – that bland, blurry backdrop on which a stain will sooner or later fall – is, from the very first, disturbingly monotonous, unsettlingly normal. The book recounts the distorted, unsociable lives of a pair of twins with no hair, eyelashes or eyebrows who, like white spectres, run a boarding house. Although lines of make-up and high-quality wigs mask the sadness of these spinsters who have grown up protected by shadows, they cannot avoid that terrible, mobile, all-too-present mirror offered by the other sister's tragedy: 'Can you shatter your twin in the same way you shatter a mirror?'

Having had her fill of watching life pass by outside the window, the day comes when one of the twins eclipses the other's reflection. The siblings silently fight over a new boarder, an affable, home-loving man who shows interest in them both because he thinks they are the same person; in such circumstances the ideal way to get the better of the other is by hiding her wig. It is a delicate operation: until then their lives have been interchangeable, and the manoeuvre – that step which is in fact a leap into the abyss – introduces an asymmetry, a crack, a betrayal with unsuspected consequences. The dispute comes to an abrupt end. Murder, that old imponderable of the best-laid plans, clears the path for a changing of roles. It is the

A FASHIONABLE LADY
in DRESS & UNDRESS.

Robert Dighton, *A Fashionable Lady in Dress and Undress*, 1807, satirical print. As a form of 'before-and-after' vignette, the bald twins of *The Flying Wig* are their own mirrors.

relegated twin who collects her sister's freshly curled wig. But death usually has no effect on hair – or at least not false hair. Transformed into an instrument of torture, the wig weighs down on the surviving twin's head like a noose of remorse. Later, it floats airily, a decapitated phantom, a guilty rodent, seeking revenge.

This perhaps minor novel would make a wonderful film in the hands of Polanski or Švankmajer. Its roots are all in fear. Not only does the twins' congenital defect act as a counterpoint to the aversion for all things hirsute – the hair-raising crevice behind the mania for depilation and the Gillette – but there is also the persecutory theme of the double. The twins, without the shadow of the wig, are as white as a sick person's tongue and suggest the melancholy of the naked mannequin. The daily scenes of dressing and undressing, thanks to the false eyelashes and the wig, the pencil with which they draw in their eyebrows, link them to a simulation of the human. Beyond the fact that Margaret is the pain-filled reflection of Amelia, and vice versa, they are both the other face of beauty, the cancer we do not want to see, the open wound of the incomplete. Monsters for each other, they end by making our hairiness, those possibly vegetal excrescences that flower on our bodies, something close to an aberration and a shudder.

Musical Curls

L ong before the Beatles made hair a symbol of rebellion
in music – the mark of a shaggy generation that, faced
with the bald heads and sleek quiffs of their elders, shakes its
locks in a rhythmical 'no' – other musicians had prepared the
way for a compositional liberation that, due to the strange links
between sonorous material and hair, directly involves coiffures.

Joseph Haydn – as a long-standing member of the Esterházy
household, he both enjoyed and suffered the discomforts of
living among servants as just another lackey – was the last great
composer to regularly wear a wig. His most outstanding pupils,
Mozart and Beethoven, who learned more from his work than
the brief lessons he was able to give them, set aside that accessory, that tangled mesh of codes that connects music to tradition
and wealth, in search of an independent style – and, naturally,
of an independent life – that would be reflected in their welcome
into the guild of Romanticism.

Lully, Bach, Handel and Vivaldi all wore sumptuous, richly
curled wigs that seemed to float like clouds arranged *en canon*.
Although it would be rash to describe their music by allusion
to the luxuriance of their wigs, it is almost impossible not to
connect it to the rituals of the nobility they served; while sacred
elements are involved in the formal beauty of their works, they
still fall within the confines of elegance and diversion in which

Thomas Hardy, *Joseph Haydn*, 1791, oil on canvas.

their art belongs: music was once described as an accompaniment to the gigantic yawns of the *ancien régime*. Haydn's wig might appear different, shorter, more stylish, but it still responds to the courtly spirit in which music is synonymous with distinction: a polished jewel of sound and tempo, an intangible sceptre of excellence and social pre-eminence. It is no coincidence that, in his contract as 'house master' of the Esterházy family, in conjunction with his duties as a musician (the document states that the prince retains exclusive ownership and copyright of the works, and that they can only be performed outside his circle as a *courtesy*), the young composer promises to care for his appearance and that of the musicians in his charge, and swears to remain faithful to the wig.

The figure of the musician-lackey is double-edged, ambiguous: Haydn complained of his isolation and 'servitude', but he had a small orchestra at his disposal with whom he could freely experiment and perform his works the day after they were composed. That enviable privilege, which due to incarceration and isolation from other composers left him no other recourse than originality, contrasts with Mozart's resistance to playing the role of servant, with all the economic instability and even poverty his emancipation entailed. The ideal of a new, itinerant, free musician who plays and composes, not for the nobility but the public – for the burgeoning middle class and their concert halls – or, as Beethoven would later declare, not even for them, but for the possibly more receptive ears of posterity, involved ridding himself of that hairy fetish that makes no secret of its ancestry, its Churrigueresque associations with power.

Due to his irreverent and difficult nature, but above all because he thought of himself as a musical entrepreneur rather than a simple servant who dines with the cooks, Mozart was expelled from, literally kicked out of, the Salzburg court. In his new incarnation, which he adopted with the mischievous enthusiasm of a free spirit and the self-confidence of a prodigy, he no longer had to pay tribute to sovereigns. While he never completely managed to avoid patronage, his abrupt departure from court changed the perception he had of himself and his art, which could then evolve in a freer, possibly déclassé but never lower sphere, an art that he could offer to the highest bidder.

At a capillary level, Mozart's rebellion was as incipient and limited as his adventures outside the ruins of feudalism. While 'Papa' Haydn, with his stiff, slightly anachronistic wig, was making his fortune in London (on a triumphal tour, with the permission of Nicholas II), the disobedient Amadeus – who refused to waste money on wigs but paid his barber huge sums to make the best of his own corn-coloured locks – beached up on the shores of debt and ill health: proof that the structure of

Portrait of Wolfgang Amadeus Mozart by Joseph Lange, Mozart's brother-in-law.

Tom Hulce
as Mozart in
Amadeus (1984),
directed by
Miloš Forman.
In the film, after
trying on three
wigs that he
loves, Mozart
exclaims with
a smile: 'Why
don't I have
three heads?'

the music market was not yet solid enough to guarantee his
independence. If the hairpiece is above all a symbol, the era did
not seem ready for a definitive de-wigging of its capillary trad-
itions, for the liberation of locks from their courtly ribbons; there
are many portraits of Mozart wearing a wig still in existence,
but towards the end of his life he added nothing more to his
loose hair than the obligatory pigtail. While he succeeded in

forswearing the wig, given his appearance and elegance of dress, anyone would have laid odds that the genius who would finally be interred on the outskirts of Vienna, in a sad, third-rate funeral, was just one more courtier.

The ritual wig, the powdered wig, would not have found its place in the attic of musical history without Ludwig van Beethoven's ostentatiously provocative irruption on the scene. Through a form of music that abhors any idea of ornament, that achieves its intensity beyond the sphere of the pastime and dedicates itself to a quest that can only be described as spiritual, Beethoven became the conduit that allowed a glimpse of a new sensibility and led to the wonderfully expanded horizons of Romanticism. But the authentic revolution that set music on its head and transformed mere noble refinement into an impassioned commitment to spiritual nobility in turn brought about a change of attitude and apparel in relation to courtly behaviour and the concept of patronage as existential servitude. At the first performance of his Symphony No. 9, Beethoven appeared in a daring green frock coat, with the dishevelled, arrogantly and unmistakably leonine mane that would become his trademark; as if its disorder, its freedom, its clear contrast to the affected and by then distant wig were also, as in the case of Schiller's 'Ode to Joy', a declaration of principles.

In the year of Haydn's death, when Beethoven's image – not just his music – was already legendary and circulated throughout Europe like the centre of a cult that related the genius's untidy appearance to the impetuous originality of his music, the German composer declined an invitation to join the court in Westphalia, something which, in his indomitable eyes, would have been the equivalent of abandoning his principles and

Edward Francis Burney, *Amateurs of Tye-wig Music (Musicians of the Old School)*, c. 1820, oil on canvas.

shouldering the never innocent yoke of the wig.[*] (Beethoven did accept the support of three aristocratic benefactors, but without a hierarchical relationship being involved, much less capillary clauses.)

If Haydn had been the first composer to achieve success outside the gilded cage of the court, it cannot be said that he composed with an eye to the nascent middle-class audiences who praised his work abroad. Beethoven, in contrast, composing for the future, turning his back on a public that demanded increasing levels of pot-pourri and fewer long, demanding works,

---

[*] Naturally, chance is involved here, but all that remains of the cult of those three great musicians in relation to melomaniac relics are a few locks of Mozart's and Beethoven's hair, cut while they were still alive or on their deathbeds (Russell Martin recounts the tangled fate of one of them in *Beethoven's Hair*). Despite the huge number of his devotees, it had never occurred to anyone to snip a lock from Haydn's wig.

inverted the social order and obliged the aristocracy to leave their castles for the first time and face the music, to visit concert halls to listen to his art, give him standing ovations and, at the peak of their enthusiasm, take off their hats and even wigs in gestures of reverence.

Capillary Plagiarism

Like the sacrifice of a virgin or the gruesome theft of a corpse, before the synthetic revolution, as a general rule the hair of a wig had belonged to a person. Although some were made from horsehair and even vegetable fibre – like the palm leaf wigs of ancient Egypt – a newly purchased wig shows the signs of an intrusive, sometimes hair-raising presence: not so much the telltale body of artificiality as the aura of a profane relic.

Whether from the desire for innovation or pure and simple baldness, during their ritual of reinvention, devotees of others' hair note that someone else very soon makes an appearance, a featureless someone else, closely resembling a mannequin or a ghostly hat stand, that offers them the possibility of achieving a faithful, lifelike appearance each morning, and then, from this side of the mirror of identity, being themselves.

For the Latin poets, the otherness of the wig was a motive for wit, and Suetonius recounted the capillary misadventures of Otho, the emperor who abused razors. In a page of *The Lives of the Caesars*, he explains that while a greater part of the world lay under Otho's dominion, his hair escaped his control and, almost bald, he had recourse to the expedient of wearing false locks, despite his obsessive shaving of the rest of his body. His receding hairline only appeared on bronze coins as he reserved his favourite, falsified appearance, his perfected image, for silver and gold.

In *The Art of Love*, Ovid does not pass up the chance to taunt women who strut like peacocks in bought locks, and Martial ridicules hair that is painted in oil or simply scattered on the vast canvas of the forehead, even going so far as to compare false hair with the practice of plagiarism: that, for him, pernicious, censurable form of cunning which allows one to incorporate the turns of phrase of another into a text as one might take possession of their curls. While Ovid wrote of the shame of being admired for something that does not belong to you:

> Now Germany will send you some slave-girl's hair;
> a vanquished nation shall furnish thy adornments.
> Alas, how oft, when thou shalt hear men praise the
> beauty of thy hair, wilt thou tell thyself with a blush,
> 'Tis purchased merchandise that makes me comely in
> their sight to-day; of some unknown Sygambrian girl
> my friends the praises sing. Yet I remember the day
> when that glory was my own.

Martial, more insidious and mocking, more concerned about literary falsification, questions in his *Epigrams* the propriety of the person who purchases or borrows hair or poems – *sui generis* merchandise, if such a thing exists – without permission, and yet aspires to something greater than feigned applause or artificial laurels.

Ovid's sophisticated, playful humour, which in *Amores* can be confused with cynicism, takes an unexpected turn when he makes the wig the target of his venom. Not even his double-edged but ultimately cruel comments on the borrowed beauty of hairpieces, the dangers of cosmetic debility, could prepare him for the love he came to feel for Julia, an overly effusive reader who had the disadvantages of being directly related to Augustus, was something of an exhibitionist, promiscuous and, to top it all, bald. Ignoring the fact that, ironically, her beauty sprang from a wig (described by some as exquisite), the poet was unable to resist her charms; in the end, it was not his libertine verses but that affair, or the awkward incidents it gave rise to – he was accused of being the 'teacher of obscene adultery' – that were secretly behind the emperor's decision to condemn him to icy exile in distant Tomis. There, isolated and suffering indigestion due to his new diet, between poems about his *Tristia*, his sadness, gazing hopelessly out over the Black Sea, he would have more

Bust of a Roman woman wearing a diadem wig, *c.* AD 80.

than enough time to reflect on the treacherous enchantments of false hair.

The fact that the wig is the trigger for quips and witticisms can be explained by the age old, possibly so slender as to be imperceptible, thread linking a hairy scalp to sarcasm. The word comes from the Greek *sarx* (flesh, body) and is related to the custom of skinning or scalping an enemy warrior in order to cover oneself with the loot (a patchwork garment sometimes taken from several foes) and so flaunt the victory. The comparison between the wig and plagiarism, however, was discovered by Martial, the poet of choler and stark humour, an undisputed genius of other varieties of flaying and misery.*

On making the text a body, and after appealing to a sense of rectitude in which the concepts of self and the original are significantly merged, the Roman satirist pours scorn on whatever is added, superimposed, never completely incorporated:

> *To Fidentinus, a Plagiarist* (Book 1, LXXII)
> Do you imagine, Fidentinus, that you are a poet by the
> aid of my verses, and do you wish to be thought so? . . .
> You too, in the same way that you are a poet, will have
> flowing locks when you are grown bald.

---

* This vein of wit was taken up by, for example, Francisco de Quevedo in his burlesque poems, where he launches an attack on sad, bald men who, at risk of seeming impolite, never take off their hats to a lady but, under threat of greater mockery, do not have the courage to sample the advantages of the wig: 'I don't have to put on wigs for my living / and since my brainbox has four white paws / my hat serves as a head.' In other poems, such as 'The bald man who neither wants to don a wig nor grow hair', he earnestly defends the dignity of those who resist pinching other people's hair. (The now-out-of-use Spanish verb *encabellarse* is defined as 'grow hair or put on a wig'.)

As a metaphor for sterility, baldness is nothing more than a variant on the atavistic conception of hair as a symbol of strength, a reflection of abundance and fertility, an association that the bellicose Martial carried into the field of literature. His interest in these matters is not incidental; he is also attributed with the figure of kidnapping (*plagium*) to represent the copying and misattribution of texts, since he was frequently the victim of these practices, and in Rome the term was used to describe the custom of making excessive use of another's slave or, more tenuously, the plan to achieve that end. Following the poet's weave of images, playing with flowing locks of appropriation, falsity and author-ship – that oblique procedure, that forged transverse warp – the plagiarist would appear to be the owner of what he does not pos-sess, with the constant risk of his falsehood being uncovered: the wig will eventually slip or fall, betrayed by poor-quality glue, an excess of sweat or even a gust of wind, revealing a deforested reality with its sheen of envy and impotence.

With reference to the wig, the trope of the plagiarized head of hair might be thought exaggerated, but Martial put his finger on the never easily assimilated presence of the *other*, on the ambi-guity of the borrowing about to be uncovered, on the shadow of the trickery in an operation that is not merely cosmetic. Perhaps Martial forgot that, with respect to the body (but also the text), what we consider to be enchantment also furnishes bewitchment, and that the battle between simulation and the authentic article is only unleashed on the hirsute scalp when we resign ourselves to the dictates of nature. When all is said and done, the catego-ries of appearance and being are relative and changeful when the body is not seen as a fixed entity – as *evidence* – but is accepted as a construction: something unfinished, material for invention,

Auguste Joliet after Horace Castelli, *Native Americans and Scalped-bald Settler*, c. 1880, engraving depicting Native Americans perplexed by the wig of one of their captives.

in which can be included the amalgam, the graft and, of course, the mask.

In terms of others' hair, as with others' texts, everything can perhaps be reduced to the success of the effect. What nature does not offer, the wig lends. And just as Michel de Montaigne confessed to the refined habit of incorporating phrases that did not belong to him into his writing – 'reasons, comparisons, and arguments . . . I transplant . . . into my own soil, and confound them amongst my own' – in the field of experimentation on the body, where authenticity is just a veneer of superstition, where erasing the boundaries between the original and what is added does not even achieve the condition of a creative act, anything transplanted into the home soil of the head can give admirable results, primarily for those who reinvent themselves before the mirror. What is reflected there – what we project to others – is as much a part of artistic elaboration and appropriation as writing, since at times a long detour through the non-self is necessary to arrive at oneself. At times a little fun and games with the other is needed to find the self.

A final note on satire. What would happen if the enemy's scalp turned out to be adorned with a wig? That was exactly what Montaigne sought when he assimilated many foreign bodies, many copied phrases, into his book: 'I will have them give Plutarch a fillip on my nose, and rail against Seneca when they think they rail at me.' Like the fate of the biblical Absalom imagined by ancient wigmakers, where, in contrast to finding his hair entangled in the branch of a tree in mid-flight, he succeeds in escaping due to the fluke of wearing a toupee ('Oh, Absalom, your capture wouldn't have mattered a fig / if only you had been wearing a wig'), sarcasm is a double-edged knife: it can detach hairpieces from where trophies were expected.

The Indiscreet Charm of Hair

Anchored as we are to routine and regularity, with the expectation that nothing will change – or at least not abruptly – even in the shifting provinces of the body, the question is always the same: what have you done to your hair?

A spurious mark of identity, a lowbrow feature that lends itself to disguise, hair is the opening lines of the spoken portrait. If the portrait is of a loved one, the first thing to be mentioned is what might be lost – or cut or dyed; superficiality and, one might say, frivolity are not necessarily equivalent to shoddiness. From this side of the witchery of the fetish it is impossible to deny the splendour of a mane of hair, its air of erotic talisman, its citizenship of the realm of enchantment. Why have years and years of natural selection ended in a penchant for hair and its expressive qualities, in the eternal frenzy for new coiffures?

The visible structures of the skin, whether hair or nails, scales or spines, horns or feathers, are known as *phaneros*, from the Greek φανερὰ (phanera) meaning manifest. These phaneros are part of the body but, more importantly, are its manifestations: they make up the most external and distinctive parts of that body, what is both a protection and allows itself to be seen. Due to their colouring and durability, their ambiguous relationship to death, they are the raw materials of taxidermy: they can be used to reconstruct the whole subject, model it as threatening or seductive, the primary poses of display and exuberance in the natural world.

As forms of epidermal animality, evolutionary excrescences for surviving climatic conditions, phaneros tend towards enormity. In humans, unsuitable subjects for dissection due to their capillary scarcity, a head of hair is a crowning phanero, the most visible and attractive external feature, the emissary of every variety of symbolism. Although we now scarcely recognize its animal ancestry, although its call has to be revived with streams of hot air, hair can be as splendid – and, possibly, strange – as a peacock's tail or a rhinoceros's horn, all varieties of keratin.

Whether it is a matter of a chameleon's scales or the feathers of a macaw, a moose's antlers or windswept hair, the question of the benefits of their anatomical design is always incomplete if limited to the need to survive, ignoring the seductive potential. We have lost the greater part of our body hair, the badge of our mammalian affiliation, but have gained a malleable mane that will never stop growing. Hair is a protection from the sun and, no less importantly, attracts potential mates; there is a reason why we spend so much time brushing and trimming it, setting it with gel like some kind of ephemeral sculpture, as if nothing were more important than offering beauty an ally. A prodigious display of the body is followed by copulation or, at very least, acceptance into the herd: the mirror can testify that we do not groom ourselves only to please those with whom we would like to have sexual relationships.

John Updike once wrote about the universe of phaneros. In a *sui generis* text for *National Geographic*, he reflected on the formidable appearance of dinosaurs, with their wealth of appendages and morphological excess: highly unusual collars that are no use for fighting, crests that would fall to pieces at the first blow, tubular excrescences that inhibit breathing. Is it any wonder that the dinosaurs became extinct? But if fossil remains make fables pale by comparison, and suggest the ridiculous anatomical pilot schemes of a primitive, experimental era, the notion that the great reptiles were the dominant species on the planet for millions of years sends astonishment over the edge of a dizzyingly high cliff. Updike suggests that the perpetuation of genes is behind a fantastic prodigality of awe-inspiring wastefulness: to judge by the plumage of present-day birds, strutting their stuff is on a par with intimidation. According to palaeontologists, dinosaur feathers were an aid to mating before they became involved in flight, and something not far removed from claws, as in an amorous embrace, would explain the disproportionately short arms of the Tyrannosaurus rex.

The sexual attraction aroused by phaneros has made them a symbol of brutality and vileness; for this reason, Satan has a great number of them, sometimes in absolute disorder, like extroversions of his profound darkness or of evil incarnate. The Devil, like the good dandy, has no lack of resources when it comes to offering temptation: the old masters used to paint him with every imaginable variety of epidermal structures copied from the animal kingdom. As if incapable of hiding his bestiality, Satan employs a fluctuating display of hooves, scales and tails to enthral us. What else is he but the great seducer who turns his back on metaphysics, the prince of all things material who defies the other world, the unrepentant libertine

Lucifer accompanied by several demons, all displaying a wide variety of phaneros, illustration in the medieval manuscript *Livre de la Vigne nostre Seigneur*, 15th century, Bodleian Library MS. Douce 134, folio 98r.

who laughs in the face of eternal condemnation in the name of material lust?*

As an accomplice to human coquetry we have privileged hair over nails or teeth. Whether eyebrows or lashes, beards or moustaches, sideburns or ringlets, we take full advantage of our hairy excrescences to attract attention. Birds swell their dewlaps or fan out their splendid plumage; we, with only occasional patches of hair (random strands scattered over what looks like chicken skin), manipulate these attributes, this contingent inheritance of the species, in what might be called desperation.

Beneath any conscious symbolism or association, we respond to the ancestral call of hair. To attract gazes, courtship insists on shaking or openly signalling it. Fingers unintentionally play with its ends or ruffle it to produce movement and volume; there is little doubt that sexual conquests would be more problematic if we were one day to wake as hairless as frogs. Perhaps because its function as a lure was all too evident, the sculpted curl in the centre of the forehead went out of fashion, but mascara never did. Under the hypnotic trance of phaneros, it was natural for eyes to be supplemented and emphasized, to the heights of extravagance, by the use of every variety of both ephemeral and permanent art: pre-prepared lashes and tattoos, perforations and implants, make-up and induced deformities.

What the plume and featherwork once signified for power and intimidation, hairpieces carried into the domain of sexual innuendo. There, where the key verb is to *impress*, borrowings and body-enhancers, the wig included, soon multiplied. In the

---

* An almost devilish marginal note: the biomolecule keratin that is the basis of phaneros (from majestic antlers to almost imperceptible bodily hair) is particularly rich in sulphur.

human body, when naked or divested of spectacular phaneros, what is self becomes confused with other and transmutations and hilarious experimentation occur. There is little point in asking which came first – the lack of a pelt or fur clothing – when artifice is a natural attribute of the species. From simulated blushes to high-heeled shoes, from the toupee to false nails, from spectacles to nylon stockings, the body does not end in that smooth, delicate skin sometimes called 'unfledged'. (The fact that later, in the harsh light of the morning after, once desire has died down, everything seems different, less splendid and suggestive is another matter. The veils are pulled back, illusions vanish, the body thought to be irresistible is nothing more than an exhausted human animal seen in a not necessarily flattering light . . . There was a reason why, in an attempt to find a material basis for enchantment and arousal, what in its moment seems like a new epiphany of Aphrodite and disturbs and sweeps away willpower, the hedonist philosophers of antiquity – with Epicurus and Lucretius at the forefront – used the notion of the *simulacrum*, the bodily emanations that directly affect the senses, dizzying them, snatching them away.)

For immediate survival, but particularly in the interminable dance of seduction – which ensures long-term survival – the human animal constructs its own phaneros, seeks to take charge of the simulacra, to augment, emphasize and even mark them on its skin with needles and fire; it borrows them from other species and carries them away in a suitcase. Any natural history of beauty must begin with phaneros and their concomitant mating dances and songs.

In contrast to animal taxidermy, where the artificial simply reinforces the mimicry – two marbles for eyes and a tongue of

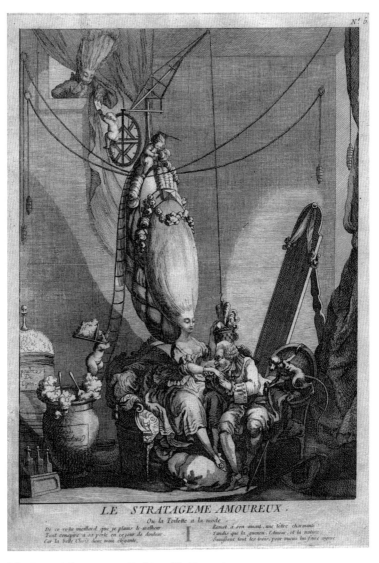

LE STRATAGEME AMOUREUX.

Ou la Toilette a la mode.

De ce vieux vieillard que je plains le malheur   Remet à son amant, une lettre charmante.
Tout conspire à sa perte en ce jour de douleur.   I   Tandis que la quenou: l'Amour, et la nature.
Car la belle Cloris bien mau élégante.   S'unissent tout les trois, pour mieux lui faire injure.

The Lovers' Strategy; or, Fashionable Grooming, c. 1775, anonymous satirical print showing a Frenchwoman being kissed by her elderly husband, while a procession of cupids climb a ladder along her ridiculously tall coiffure to deliver letters to her young lover above.

painted plaster – the embalming of people (or, in some cases, their wax replicas) is not complete until all the features of their public appearance, including prostheses and cosmetics, have been incorporated. The embalmed corpse of an important politician or movie star is not fit to be seen without its characteristic hairstyle, clothes and jewels. Or, if necessary, its toupee or ostentatious pigtail.

Beautys Lot.

Adorn'd with Tates, I well could Boast, Of Tons and Macaronys Toast;
I once was Fair, Young, Frisky, Gay, Could please with songs and Dance the Hay.
Dear Bells reflect Ye Mortals see, As I now am, so You will be.
Pub in the Air'streets by Wᵐ Humphrey 227 S'trand Lavion

The contrast between the skull and the wig as a memento mori.
Beautys Lot, 1778, English print satirizing the macaroni fashion.

On Remains and Other Relics

Just a single hair, if it has become detached or is in an inappropriate place, is capable of producing disgust, recoil and sometimes horror. When it is in soup, on the tip of one's tongue or clinging to a bar of soap, hair loses its symbolic enchantment and is merely waste matter. It can be included in the category of the lowest of the low, something that must be removed, the further away the better. Although it is not subject to the same process of decomposition as other body parts, it is a representative of 'bare life', a loose thread of our organic skein – of what Aristotle called *zoe* – and, for that reason, a furtive emissary of death. That awakening in which the pillow has become a spine-chilling canvas à la Jackson Pollock streaked by hair loss announces illness and the feared decline.

A tangle of hairs, like those swept up every evening in a hairdresser's or barber's shop, anticipates the monstrous; the threat that it might acquire a life of its own. Simultaneously body and debris, the sudden manifestation of fear, it is the remnant of something we believed forgotten, an eminently mammalian shudder we initially battle against in those pagan temples known as beauty salons.

Along with our bones, teeth and nails, hair survives us. It is commonly believed that it goes on growing after death, as if it hadn't noticed or were an efflorescence, a parasitic plant of the epidermis. When we are reduced to dust, the mane of hair remains in all its splendour, glossy and undulating if exposed to the wind, in a disquieting nod to eternity. A conspicuous mass of last remains, the gloomy cluster that acts as a bookmark, it is the most intimate, the most emblematic of our relics; perhaps even more so than the skull, and without which we would be unrecognizable at first glance. If one can talk of some sense of posthumous beauty, this resides in the hair, which preserves its gloss and colour for centuries.

Examples exist of hair that is more than 3,000 years old (such as on the mummified body of Ramesses II), and since time immemorial locks and whole braids have been conserved (in caskets, lockets or miniature temples) and, rather than producing repulsion, have become objects of adoration. The discovery of a lock of hair in a small box, which horrifies anyone taken unawares, could be the fetish of some former lover who did not succumb to witchcraft. From a mere excrescence and residue, subterranean booty for ants, it becomes the depository of meanings: an erotic trophy, a testimony of loss, an instrument of voodoo, the mark of God incarnate.

In addition to its role as a talisman or an extension of the person in magic tricks, hair can be found among the principal relics of the Catholic Church's saints and martyrs, in the rather dubious rubric of 'first-class' (those that were once part of the body in contrast to others that gained sacred status due to mere proximity or contact). In Sangüesa, Spain, one can (supposedly) find a hair belonging to Mary Magdalene and another to the Virgin Mary, both problematic relics if we attend to Paul the Apostle (Saul of Tarsus), who warns that female hair emits some type of devil in the form of sparks, the reason for his decree that women should cover their heads at all times, as did Jewish wives. Whether they are authentic or not, these biblical leftovers prove that what we cast off in secular life can change its symbolism and become a motive for pilgrimage.

At the opposite end of the spectrum from the hair within a shrine is its placement in a romantic museum. There are examples of collections of scented ringlets, plaits of hair sacrificed for love and, of course, curious cabinets of pubic hair. Giacomo Casanova once had sugar-coated pills prepared from essences and strands of hair sent to him by a beautiful woman. Ground to facilitate the lewd alchemy of the confectionary, the strands delighted the lover so much that he swallowed them each morning and night, not as a love potion but as a stand-in for or anticipation of what he was certain to later sample.

Lord Byron, a somewhat cloying version of the eighteenth-century gallant who made his conquests in a wig and cape, was in the habit of meticulously preserving hairy relics of his encounters in individual envelopes, as a form of restoring the effective presence of Venus to the act of veneration. He boasted of having seduced more than two hundred women during his stay in Venice alone – that swampy city has always been an invitation to amatory prowess – so that it is easy to imagine the wide variety of his harvest, somewhere between hunting trophies and gallant souvenirs. In 1980 the trail of his portable museum was lost; its last resting place seems to have been his publishing house in London. 'Dead scandals form good subjects for dissection,' wrote Byron, possibly conscious that he would suffer that fate one day.

Luisa Futoransky, the shorn and captivating author of *Pelos* (Hair), visited the collection of a certain Swiss professor who,

Lock of John Lennon's hair trimmed in preparation for filming the 1967 comedy *How I Won the War*. The substantial lock was preserved and sold by Klaus Baruck, his hairdresser in Hamburg, Germany.

Lock of Marilyn Monroe's hair, preserved and sold by her personal hairdresser, Kenneth Battelle.

at the end of the nineteenth century and with the assistance of several generations of his students, replicated the project of the author of *Don Juan*, on this occasion for scientific purposes that are somewhat unclear because, beyond the clinical, professorial halo surrounding the process of the extraction of samples, it is impossible for a collection of that nature to be completely devoid of erotic charge.

In the 1970s the Spanish director Luis García Berlanga made a film based on the idea of that hirsute museum, that barefaced tribute to Venus or, more precisely, to her delicate mount. In one comic scene of *La escopeta nacional* (The National Shotgun, 1978), the frenzied daughter-in-law of the Marqués de Leguineche destroys and tramples the precious, rich heritage (preserved in test tubes and vials, labelled with the name of the donor and the number of encounters); the sight of his amatory collection, the small altar to his extracurricular activities, being stamped into the ground almost causes the already decrepit aristocrat to faint. The scene ends with his son's unforgettable remark: 'But it's bush hair!' With that cry, he demystifies and returns to the realm of filth what had passed for a treasure.

There is a risqué precedent directly linking pubic hair to the wig. In *A History of Orgies*, Burgo Partridge (who spent his childhood among the famous Bloomsbury Group) refers to Edinburgh's mid-eighteenth-century Wig Club. This order – it goes without saying that it was licentious and given to the practice of recondite erotic rituals – used to gather around a wig originally made from the pubic hair of no lesser a personage than the mistress of Charles II, a monarch with a well-known predilection for hairpieces. During the ceremony, in which steamy passages from the Song of Songs were read and one or two initiations carried out, each of the people assembled there had the right to kiss the wig and place it on his head for a short time. Moreover, the neophytes were obliged to convince their lovers to make a pubic sacrifice; thus the body of the hairpiece was not only fattened by curly strands, but continually renewed. All this was done under the tutelage of a number of monks who had no particular interest in guarding their vows of chastity and gave their solemn blessing to the congregation: go forth and multiply.*

Considered to be of lower status than flesh, and mixed among organic waste – hair and nails have a closer relationship to the rubbish bin than the coffin – a head of hair retains the identity of its owner beyond death. It gives information about his or her diet, cosmetic habits and general health – although, surprisingly, not gender – so, as might be expected, it becomes a symbol of that owner, an all the more obsessive fetish in that it takes no part in the simulacrum.

Hair, particularly if it has been preserved in the form of a coiffure, offers the body one of its most arresting manifestations, one which attracts gazes as strongly as a person's eyes. It is no small matter that, rescued from the grave, as in a story by Edgar Allan Poe, it allows itself to be caressed by the comb of the fingers.

---

* There are other references to this strange craftsmanship of the wig in which the pubic becomes public. According to Lichtenberg's notes, one day, in the euphonic locality of Brunswick, a wig made from 'the most intimate hair of a young woman' was auctioned. Obviously, the lot went for a high price.

Dressing Up Justice

Before they donned their rippling, white, horsehair wigs, British judges used to cover their heads with a flat linen cap. During the Middle Ages, the characteristic attire of magistrates included furs and silk robes whose colour varied according to the season, until black – the Solomonic uniform of arbiters – became the norm as a symbol of impartiality. The aim of all this slightly archaic, strikingly exaggerated paraphernalia, which could also include lace, spotless gloves and a host of insignias, was to leave an impression on the mind and install a ritual parenthesis, the suprahuman period of the implementation of justice. Thanks to the dispassionate theatricality of the pomp, the outlandish apparel that separates judges from the common lot and to some extent makes them unrecognizable, credibility is displaced from the individual to the personage so that sentences are handed down by atemporal, relatively unknown figures, stern puppets controlled by the imperturbable strings of duty.

But when they exercise power with an intimidating display of the body, the appearance of judges – reinforcing hierarchies through a wealth of squander – also contributes to concealing incriminating differences in the legal sphere, just as did the tonsures of monks who held posts outside the Church. The linen caps, and their curled replacements weighing several kilograms, cover up stigmata and cloak lineages; like the costume of a Rococo superhero who, instead of a cape and mask, dons false hair and a long robe, these items of apparel cover details of identity or social position that might be revealing or suggest bias.

While the wig did not become one of the emblems of justice until the early nineteenth century, when Humphrey Ravenscroft invented a practical model that did not have to be powdered and only rarely combed through, judges and barristers, as with the majority of the guilds and professions of a certain status, had already adopted their use in the mid-seventeenth century, when Charles II returned from his long exile in France having caught the fever for hairpieces. According to the studious Charles M. Yablon, known for his erudition in terms of legal wigs, their proliferation in England was as sudden and unstoppable as the plague, due, among other things, to the fact that in a society riven by the Civil War that single, hairy mantle masked old quarrels that had even encompassed hairstyles: the parliamentarians, better known as the Roundheads, wore their hair short while the royalists, or Cavaliers, sported flowing locks. And although it goes without saying that the new fashion favoured the – not necessarily neutral – bald, the use of the wig became an unexpected solution to differences and an exotic call for peace.*

The 'mature' smell of the wig – in its literal and figurative senses – provoked a reaction from the Founding Fathers of the United States, who, in a parallel gesture to the Declaration of

---

* In terms of the plague, the wig endured a great deal of distrust, often related to infection. In his *Diary*, Samuel Pepys attests to the fear that wigs could be unconscious vehicles of contagion, particularly when they were second-hand or made from the remains of victims of the plague. Naturally, fleas and nits had a great deal to do with his fear.

Independence, expressed their outright opposition to its use in court. Even though Thomas Jefferson and other revolutionaries wore wigs, they resisted the perpetuation of the symbol, which was by then rivalling the figure of the blindfolded woman holding a pair of scales and had become a detested colonial inheritance, even in the tropics, where legal affairs were often carried out in a torrid climate with the addition of plentiful sweat. When visiting a London court, Jefferson was shocked by the fact that they were presided over by people like 'rats peeping through their bunches of oakum'.

William Hogarth, *The Bench*, 1758–64, etching and engraving. Just a short step away from caricature, it depicts the distraction and ostentation of the magistrates.

The good old days of the legal wig in England, *c.* 1937.

On 12 July 2007, having sat in the dock on a number of occasions in the course of its history, and after a Byzantine four-year debate that generated powdered rancour and one or two geriatric tantrums, the wig was formally abolished in British civil courts. Modernization, and more specifically budget cuts, won out over the pure rituality of men (and women) of law, limiting the use of their traditional attire to criminal cases and specific commemorations. The scene of justice, the antediluvian antechamber to the scaffold, would still be presided over by woolly puppets in a bold bid for realism.

As a belated vindication of Jefferson, a demystifying measure involving the whole costume and not merely the majestic capillary crest, the ruling not only disrupted the forms and protocols of the law, but upset the very notion of British justice. Turning the courts into one more form of bureaucracy, stripping judges and barristers of their solemn habits, and so setting them on the same level as anyone else, involved the erasure of an ancestral tradition that had inspired respect in those accused and helped the judges of both sexes to play their roles to the full, enfolding them in a sort of professional reverie. In compensation, it returned the practice of the law to a terrestrial, less distanced and more humane level that – as with any other practice – is stalked by error, corruption and iniquity.

The judge's peruke – basically paraphernalia, an unnecessary excrescence, even if for several centuries one could not make a living without it – is a badge as dispensable as it is evocative, whose partial abolition demonstrated just how deeply society was implicated in it, was involved in the series of assumptions and meanings inscribed in its clearly artificial purity. A rather comical accessory ('peruke' is derived from *perroquet*, and from that also comes 'parakeet', indicating the pompous swagger of birds, but also the long-winded perorations of the courts), a hyperbolic exhibition of a series of values that have a tendency to vanish when taken for granted, the hairy scaffolding of the judge prefigures dispositions and responses, highly specific behaviours that, far from adding to the object in the form of a collective projection, could be said to derive from its interior like a force field.

The lustrous head of hair, which when it turns yellow enjoys the strange honour of being valued on the black market as an aristocratic trophy, induces forms of behaviour and attitudes that are not open to appeal – behaviours and attitudes that elevate it to the heights of a tangled sign: rather than the leftovers of an era with an overdeveloped sense of the ridiculous, the wig became an allegory and evocation of impartiality. No matter how uncomfortable and unhygienic, it was able to overcome its temporal lag, its anachronism, its irksome defeat, and so rise up as the investiture of rectitude and due process, even when it had already perhaps spent too many years resting on laurels in the form of ringlets.

As with the executioner's hood, which in addition to protecting his identity turns him into a simple cog in the machine, absolved from guilt – the material effect of a decision taken by the anonymous system he serves – the legal wig, that matured crest of power and privilege, is as much a mask as the propitiatory screen: it creates a world within a world, an inevitably rigid, blatantly ritual bubble outside of time that, nevertheless, through protocol, insignia and etiquette, struggles not to descend into farce.

Towering Hairdos

C ontemporary caricatures used to depict them as large enough to house a whole garden or a labyrinth – or even the man they were intended to conquer. But there was little need for exaggeration in those prints. Since hyperbole, the knife-edge of satire, was the domain and delight of the women portrayed, mockery of their coiffures was bound to reach incredible heights.

Erect as masonry menhirs, monolithic as obelisks on which to hoist chignons, as insalubrious as a viper's nest, home to the most surprising fauna, these hairstyles were so complex, so ingeniously unrestrained that, rather than a fashion, they could be said to prefigure dioramas and the concept of the World Fair.

During the decades of inequality and affectation that preceded the French Revolution, in Europe the wig literally reached its highest peak when the importance of a woman's head could be measured in the cubic centimetres of her sculpted hair. Despite its detrimental effects on the neck of the wearer (stiffness and immobility of the cervical vertebrae raised to a mark of distinction), the baroque mass grew unchecked towards the heavens to denote supremacy.* Just as with many

* The wig has been denounced on innumerable occasions for its supposed detrimental effects on health, although this condemnation

other sumptuary symbols, the value of those hairy cupolas was based on the time needed to construct them: hours and hours of sculptural leisure that converted the wearer into a luxury nuisance, a multicoloured, talking piñata.

Assisted by a structure of rods, held together by ribbons, fattened by a mane of hair and wool, bedecked with an astonishing array of fabrics, jewels, powder, feathers, fruit and scale models, the styles known as *d'apparat* (ceremonial) employed the now common strategy of adding second and third storeys to the construction for greater effect: ships, towers, temples, battles; flocks of geese, porcupines, boughs, even water . . . anything at all fitted in the capillary scaffolding created by wig-artists mounted on stilts and aided by plans and sextants – again according to the satirical prints of the time. And when the headdress was complete, it often had to be left untouched for days or even weeks (on occasion the ladies must have had to sit up all night so as not to spoil the next day's coiffure).

Those freaks eventually reached such heights that Montesquieu mockingly commented that the beauty of a female face must be exactly in the middle of an elongated figure with the nether regions composed of the body and the upper half a tower of hair in whose construction an architect was as often as not[*] involved. (If conditions ever existed for a flourishing hairpin industry, it must have been then.)

---

might be better directed at what it represents: superficiality and inauthenticity. By contrast, in 1828, in his *Art coiffer soi-même* (The Art of Hairstyling for Women), M. Villaret writes: 'The wig not only adorns the head, but gives it more strength and vigour: it prevents fluxions of the mouth, ear problems, headaches, ophthalmia, nervousness etc.; many people who suffer attacks of catarrh owe their cure to the use of a wig lined with flannel or agaric.'

THE FLOWER GARDEN.

Matthew Darly, *The Flower Garden*, 1777, etching and engraving with watercolour. Hair, an ancient symbol of fertility, is home to a flourishing miniature garden.

But the body reduced to a pedestal, a mere support for a metre and a half of insignia, is a minor detail in comparison with the audacity of directly sculpting emotions in hair. With the affected clumsiness of an encrypted language intended to awe all and sundry, sorrow, sexual innuendo, melancholy and affliction were soon encoded; the iconographic elements were as clear and emphatic as modern road signs: sarcophagi for widows, butterfly nets for frivolity and amorous adventures. A hairstyle can say more than a thousand words, particularly if it is conceived as a window to the soul.

Jean-François Autier, better known as Léonard, hairdresser and confidante to Marie Antoinette, has gone down in history as the creator of the style. However, the fashion for conquering the skies with a hairdo had in fact already enjoyed a century of outlandish excess; since the reign of the Sun King, Louis XIV, with its *fontange* coiffure (accidentally 'discovered' by one of his mistresses during an excursion to Fontainebleau), majesty had been associated with all kinds of absurd frippery, the less lifelike the better. In fact, the Leonardo of hairpieces – to whom, in the midst of revolution, the queen assigned tasks too delicate for his abilities and rank (with the apparent objective of having him available to powder her hair and care for her appearance at explosive moments, it is known that she smuggled letters in the armature of her coiffure) – was the inventor of a particular variety of capillary fantasy, the *pouf aux sentiments*, which, with the charm of its metaphorical weight, carried to extremes the premise that, when suitably groomed, hair is not just a cosmetic caprice but a microcosm.

Once the crown of the head had been transformed into an architect's model, there was no reason for it to limit itself to the representation of the universe of the mind. With the door of invention open to the animal and vegetable kingdoms, it was only to be expected that hairstyles would accommodate the industry and works of the human species. Alongside the day's anniversaries, they soon celebrated the latest news: waves of hair commemorating a naval victory – the famous *La Frégate* style – with ships floundering in the curls, or *fabulas medicas* noting the date when the royal family were inoculated against smallpox. Any event could be recorded on the wig in a personalized variant of a carnival float. In 1783, as a tribute to the Montgolfier brothers' invention, women competed to display the best hot-air-balloon hairstyle.

The eccentricity of this fashion made it subject to every imaginable difficulty, such as the risk of finding oneself caught up in a crystal chandelier or singed by candelabras. Although aristocratic women could no longer enter carriages with ease or stand upright in any room, in their determination to show off their colourful cephalic towers they decided it would be preferable to enlarge the door frames than to take a saw to a piece of capillary art: the outcome was that, according to caricatures, women were accompanied by a retinue of carpenters and builders. A certain Baulard, who should perhaps be remembered as a great inventor rather than a hairdresser, created a masterpiece that avoided such inconveniences by means of a spring-action device. The retractable wig, better known as 'the grandmother', not only rose and fell to allow for the passage of the wearer through doorways, but was a means of evading shocked scoldings from elderly relatives – hence the name – who were sometimes unprepared for an encounter with the hypertrophy of fashion.

RIDICULOUS TASTE OR THE LADIES ABSURDITY.

The architecture of the wig. Matthew Darly, *The Ridiculous Taste;
or, The Ladies Absurdity*, 1771, print satirizing the *pouf aux sentiments*
hairstyle.

Francis E. Adams, *Heyday! Is This My Daughter Anne!*, 1773, mezzotint and etching on paper. Even in London grandmothers cried out to the heavens.

In his *History of Fashion in France*, Challamel notes the inconveniences caused by these wigs in such venues as the opera, where women with a penchant for mountainous wigs were frequently to be seen. In many cases it was necessary to establish strict rules: women with pharaonic headdresses that exceeded a specified height were prohibited for fear they would block the view of others. But as ladies were reluctant to attend theatres and other social venues without their mind-boggling *poufs*, news spread of foreigners who, incapable of suppressing their impatience and disconcertion, threw shoes or whatever else came to hand at their neighbour's pyramid, some of which could easily be mistaken for fluttering forests of feathers.

While there is no way of measuring the importance of humour in the spirit of a nation, the avalanche of satirical prints based on these colossal chimeras would lead one to think that, in addition to being extremely expensive and highly impractical, they were all-too-visible symbols of wealth and overly audacious crests of injustice. Preserved in great quantities in the Musée Carnavalet and the Bibliothèque Nationale in Paris, those caricatures of haughty power, those scathing depictions of conspicuous superficiality, did perhaps in their moment contribute to bringing social unrest to boiling point. When artists drew gardeners mounted on step-ladders attempting to prune the foliage of a coiffure or hunters 'mistakenly' shooting the stuffed birds in a lady's hair, what else were they doing but uncovering the unlikely stage machinery of opulence? Behind their critique of manners was a political barb. Although Marie Antoinette herself contributed to calming the rage for this hirsute version of gigantism when she suffered hair loss after giving birth and set the fashion for hair tied at the nape of the neck, her fate might have been very different if she had not been enticed by the delirious inventions of Monsieur Léonard, the wizard of fantasy hairstyles.

The imposing mounds of hair, those authentic aerial museums that would have been the envy of Carmen Miranda, very soon became the target of attacks and the pretext for egalitarian uprisings. Dangerous in their ostentation, double-edged swords that attracted the attention of both accomplices and enemies, their reign ended under the sibilant lightning flash of the guillotine.

'The Revolutionary cannonballs', Francisco Barado concludes in his *Historia del peinado* (A History of Hairstyles), 'that pierced the walls of the Bastille, reducing them to rubble, also demolished the pyramids erected by coquetry on the heads of women.' His statement echoes many others of the same variety, particularly one offered by Montesquieu in his *Persian Letters*, where, with visionary perspicacity and his unmistakable touch of black humour, the author seems, seventy years before the queen's execution, to be aware of the political consequences of extravagance and capillary folly: 'Sometimes the headdresses grow gradually to a great height, until a revolution brings them down suddenly.'

Abbé de Choisy; or, the Inner Woman

A courtier, historian, musician and occasional actor who continued to play roles offstage, the Abbé de Choisy was involved in such novel undertakings as being one of the first French ambassadors to Siam, but he is best known as a brilliant cross-dresser. His mother, who hosted a very popular salon and was responsible for educating the future Louis XIV in the courtly arts (and possibly also those of the bedchamber), decided to dress him as a woman until the age of eighteen, less as a whim or perversion than as part of a complex intrigue. Philippe, Duke of Orléans, the younger brother of the king, significantly nicknamed *Monsieur*, had a penchant for the voluptuousness of cross-dressing; when he found Madame de Choisy's home to be a safe and agreeable place to give free rein to his interest, the risk of scandal put an end to what few political ambitions he possessed. It fell to the youngest of the Choisy brothers – François Timoléon – to be his accomplice, and from an early age the boy learned to eradicate any sign of masculinity from his body.

In 1666, aged 22, still with a child's complexion thanks to an incredible but apparently effective cocktail ('veal water and sheep's-foot pomade'), Choisy found himself with an explosive inheritance: money in abundance, an ecclesiastic education at the Sorbonne and the pleasure of walking the

François Timoléon, abbé de Choisy, as a woman,
illustration in *Musée des familles: Lectures du soir*,
vol. XXII (1854–5).

fine line of gender ambiguity. Encouraged by Madame de La Fayette, and with his mother's wardrobe at his disposal, Choisy decided to exchange his soutane for skirts and his tonsure for exotic hairstyles. Although he did indeed present himself as a woman at a number of public events, with a boldness that reveals his confidence in his charms (it is said that in Rome he attended a ball celebrating the coronation of the Pope dressed as a *grande dame*, and in the diplomatic mission in Siam the locals put his over-elaborate appearance down to some outlandish Occidental custom), Choisy chose to move to a quiet neighbourhood on the outskirts of Paris. There, living incognito, possessor of a fortune capable of financing the theatre of appearance, he not only lavished money on his 'bagatelles', adorning himself with corsets, earrings and wigs, but reinvented himself from head to toe. That was when, at the prime of life, Madame de Sancy was born; a dazzling, enigmatic woman who carried her incorrigible need to be loved to the extreme of leaving both men and women breathless.

In his *Memoirs*, which anticipate and at times eclipse those of Casanova – another dissolute abbé with a taste for disguise – Choisy writes with elegance and amenity, in a confidential tone that allows him to digress time and again without the reader worrying about losing the thread, and where the change to the feminine form of nouns and adjectives is as imperceptible as the shadow on his chin, about the origins of what he terms his 'extravagant pleasures'. With guilt-free *savoir faire*, the exact opposite of the paranoid ravings of Daniel Paul Schreber (that judge with several mental ailments who wanted to become a woman and triggered no less delirious comments

from celebrated psychoanalysts; for Jacques Lacan, by contrast, Choisy illustrates the amazing genius of 'perfect
perversion'), the abbé writes that there is no more insistent
human urge than the desire to be loved – from which not even
God is exempt – and that, on finding in himself traces of beauty
capable of awakening that love, he simply followed his natural
inclinations, enhancing that beauty with adornments and
coquetry that favoured his female side. He admits that his
deepest passion is to be loved; that when he passes by, the
excitement and erotic tension bring everything to a halt; that
he sees on people's lips the word-talisman, the priceless piece
of flattery that repays all his efforts: *Mademoiselle!*

Sainte-Beuve, who appreciated the seriousness of the
future well-known author, depicts him in a way that makes
one think of a continual short circuit: 'From his earliest
childhood he wore the tonsure of priesthood, but his mother
appears to have principally dedicated him to female finery.
As vain as a nun in Vert Vert, and as garrulous as a parrot.'

Slave to his desires, determined that his dual sexuality
should not impose restrictions on him, Choisy embraced the
cause of sexual freedom with the temerity of someone who
has expunged the word 'reputation' from the dictionary.
Distanced from the strictly controlled environment of the
court, he dedicated himself to captivating young women
whom, to complete the masquerade, he persuaded to dress
'en garçon'. Enthralled by the fiction that made him feel a 'real
woman', by the fatal elytra of mimesis – wigs, ribbons, beauty
spots that aided the flight of his butterfly – his complex conquests did not satisfy him until his 'little husband', always an
innocent girl dazzled by the ostentation and prodigality of the

strange woman, could be mistaken for a man and, in the appropriate garb (waistcoat, gloves and a male wig), also become a sexual chimera.

Behind the compensatory illusion, beneath the sheets of a shared mirage that Choisy did not hesitate to call 'marriage', physiology enabled the bodies to find their own route. The cosmetic conversion – pursuing a fugitive unreality rather than gradually approaching a model – could not negate the anatomy of the lovers, but it did achieve an integration of those attributes in a ceremony in which arousal is intensified thanks to the act of transformation, to the splitting of personality and the assumed voice as passionate forms of being beyond oneself.

When the banns were about to be posted (Choisy could not resist the temptation to boast of his nuptials at the opera, where he inevitably stole the show, but also caused raised eyebrows), he changed his residence and resigned himself to the mask of a gentleman. As if he had to substitute one weakness for another, whenever the wigs and girdles were stored away in his wardrobe he fell headlong into the deep pit of gambling and, time after time, wagered his inheritance and possessions until he was ruined. If the card sharp as the other face of the coquette resembles the duplicity of a paraphilia manual, Choisy took the pendulum of restitution to the point of caricature: while he was allowed to be a woman, he censured the vice of gambling and despised those addicted to it; in that happy facet of his being, the only guiles he allowed himself were of a cosmetic nature. His abomination of cards was a frank expression of his abomination of his other life, the hatred he felt for the role society forced him to play against the grain of his desires. Although it borders on paradox, for Choisy the worst form of castration was not being able to become 'she'.*

Whether as the hypnotic Madame de Sancy or the provocative Madame La Comtesse Des Barres, Choisy paid the price for his extraordinary extroversion. The thirst for pageantry and simulation, for attracting attention at any cost – in *La simulación* (Simulation), Severo Sarduy calls this a hypertelic urge – leaves him an easy victim for infamy. The colourful unfolding of the butterfly's wings with which he seduced his partners also drew the eyes of predators – in this case, the moral variety – who did not hesitate to single him out and call him to account, even after his death; d'Alembert's tract of 1777 is in fact a bitter moralistic reproach dressed up as praise.

In an age when cross-dressing flourished in all directions and a surprising collection of clerics were fascinated by cosmetic edifices, Choisy stands out not so much for the audacity of dressing his 'perverted partners' as men, as for openly speaking of his predilection in an admirable book that is both honest and disturbing. If that 'small weakness of wanting to pass for a woman' was tolerated in his time as long as it restricted itself

---

* The most famous cross-dresser in history, the Chevalier d'Éon, who shortly after Choisy made women's clothing an accessory to espionage and was a renowned exponent of 'romantic piracy', also had good reasons for abhorring gambling. The London Stock Exchange organized a notorious betting pool on his gender that aroused so much morbid curiosity and gave rise to such astronomical wagers that it was feared the diplomat was in danger of being abducted. Even Casanova issued a verdict. A 'novice' in imposture, as he presented himself, but with first-hand experience of gender ambiguity, the Venetian libertine laid odds on the female of the species. The post-mortem showed that, at least from a merely biological viewpoint, he was wrong.

Mademoiselle de Beaumont; or, The Chevalier d'Éon, 1777, engraving.

to the sphere of amusement (and Choisy, of course, did not restrict himself: he had a daughter with one of his female-males), the uncontrollable desire to be loved, to even flaunt his metamorphosis in writing, made him fantasize about taking the matter further. The original plan of his *Mémoires pour servir à l'histoire du règne de Louis XIV* (Memoirs to Illustrate the Reign of Louis XIV), which he wrote dressed as a still attractive widow although in the capacity of a member of the Academy, included sprinkling those memories with his own adventures in female clothing, by way of a 'strange contrast'. In the end, he did not dare go so far and the two paths suffered unequal fates. While the book of collective history was applauded and reissued, its libertine counterpart, his dishevelled, shameless confession, was an affront – partly because of its exceptional merits – to the silence of censure, and was not published in full until 1862, over a hundred years after his death.

If, as François Mauriac notes, 'the century of the wig is when man has employed least disguise,' Choisy, who wore wigs of any size and for any occasion (at the beginning of his *Memoirs* he mentions six different models, practically one per page), was capable of using them to shorten the distance that separated him from himself, to bring to the surface, if only intermittently and not without censure or risk, the woman residing within him.

Cindy Sherman
in Simulationland

No one knows better than a male cross-dresser that femininity is a fascinating construction, a precarious artifice of additions and substitutions (of layers of make-up and localized enlargements, diets and diverse depilation) that women themselves constantly imitate and sometimes, in an unequal contest, battle against. Like Eves moulding the very clay from which they are made – sometimes to the limits of its malleability – many practise the daily exercise of the before-and-after photograph, that illusion systematized by advertising and the beauty dictatorship, that dressing- (and operating-) table Golem into which they attempt to breathe life each morning without worrying if the result is at times grotesque.

But male cross-dressers, as Severo Sarduy points out, neither imitate nor copy womankind; dazzled, they simulate her appearance, the effects she radiates, with a wealth of exaggeration; they are capable of having a rib removed to produce that astonished paralysis that fades as soon as it appears. In the interminable process of the construction of identity, women, on the other hand, have to confront, and sometimes turn their backs on, a series of stereotypical images of the feminine, time-honoured models and standards backed up by show business, no less tyrannical for being spectral. Whether as the puerile princess or an independent woman, an unprepossessing doll or a housewife, a matron or a femme fatale, every step on her road to individualization is subject to the tension of resembling another, to that alienating counter-play of being the image of someone else, in a range of possibilities that is, in the eyes of others – in the gaze of those who sanction and encourage the chosen role – frequently reduced to the banal polarity of the prostitute and the saint.

In the late 1970s Cindy Sherman emerged onto the contemporary art scene with a series of snapshots – the famous *Untitled Film Stills* – which, while suggesting a disturbing story in a single, one might say orphaned, shot with no before-and-after, display the delicate mechanisms that intervene in the construction of the image of the woman or, perhaps, in the still problematic construction of the woman as image. Part cross-dresser resolved to impersonate the varieties of femininity of a particular period, and part dress-art artist who wants first-hand experience of the power of that alienation without denouncing it, Sherman grasped the strings that control fictional characters – herself as countless mannequins – to, among other things, evade the question of whether they are the same strings that operate in daily life, in the confirmation of the mask.

Provisioned with wigs, period clothes and a carefully planned selection of desolate locations reminiscent of European black-and-white cinema and 1950s Hollywood noir, Sherman concocts a captivatingly vague parody, infested with ambiguity and controversy, that some have written off as a smug celebration, a scandalous perpetuation of dominant fantasies and clichés, the oppressive sexual glamour of advertising. Even if all parody is ultimately a deformed celebration, Sherman's one-frame films – that frozen cinema through which parade countless representations of (frivolous, vulnerable, determined,

Cindy Sherman, *Untitled Film Still #14*, 1978, gelatin silver print,
10 × 8 inches.

disconsolate, poorly dressed, sophisticated) women in a sort of glossary of the masquerades and gestures of a highly evocative but basically indeterminate period – not only succeed in decoding the grammar of female identities without trivializing their irreducible multiplicity, but take advantage of the symbolic power of a very few elements to paradoxically give human depth to the effigies; by doing so, Sherman questions the extent to which it is possible to brand them as peripheral, superfluous, deceitful or simply self-evident.

As nothing other than brief photo shoots with the photographer herself as the model, sham, static remakes of films that never existed, the stills nevertheless compel one to fall into the old trap of physiognomists, those decipherers of faces and other epidermal features; then, already lost in the maze of simulacra, the combination of a messy hairstyle and a neorealist top is enough to give a glimpse of the turbulence of a whole life. In the manner of Edgar Allan Poe's amateur detective, we suddenly feel capable of reading, 'even in that brief interval of a glance, the history of long years'.

The recurrence of disguise and props in Sherman's explorations produces a contrast to the aura of photography as the tool of truth par excellence. When she plays in ephemeral sets with variables of the code of appearance, she manages to make them reveal themselves, come to light, confront us with a level of estrangement and distance, as if in some way the camera were capable of stripping away the trickery or, better, as if that stage set were displaying its mechanisms without destroying the artifice. Since the material of her searches is the image – the image of the woman, the image she projects and that is projected on her face – she was wise enough to include photographic syntax (framing, illumination, depth of field, granularity and so on) as a fundamental element of the construction, as another of its innumerable layers, thanks to which what remains manifest is not only the forgotten strangeness of, for example, arranging one's hair to make it complicit in the aspirations; in addition, the ambiences, the framework of props and light, become a seductive dressing room, an effective projection of the look (each character seems to be a tribute to a director whose name we cannot remember; the timely incarnation of a style that feels familiar but never quite clear).

When Sherman includes the iconography of film, television and social stereotypes as chemicals enhancing the emulsion of her art, she is highlighting the density and also the fragility of the fiction of the I. Precisely due to the fact that she herself is the person who appears – and does not appear – chameleon-like in all the photos, we understand that choosing the appropriate hairstyle or drawing the contours of other lips over her own are steps as essential as utilizing the spirit of the location or vanishing in the mnemonic wink of déjà vu. The self and other merge into an evocative continuum in which the limits of the body are extended in every direction to include both the wig and the fabrics. Exactly because each photograph is, above all, a self-portrait, a carefully planned, nuanced self-representation, it captures the palette of elements available to her for the reinvention: the whole gamut of false hair, gestures, environments and cosmetics, on which rest her presence, her new story to be intuited in the blink of an eye.

The question of the 'true' Cindy Sherman, misguided if put to her elusive masks, takes on other aspects when directed at the parade of disguises, that long, interrupted monologue which, from behind the camera, she has carried on with her models over the years, with herself posing in the eyepiece of a kaleidoscope, on both sides of the optical aperture of the same recurrent phrase: 'Nobody wants to be just what she already is.'

Even though she forces the spectator to observe through the peephole of the voyeur (her photographs simultaneously arouse curiosity and an erotic charge, features not always concurrent with desire), in the possibilities of her spectacle, Sherman does not come across as a narcissist; when she reflects herself in the cracked mirror of the self, she succeeds in producing a challenge, a crevice of perplexity; when she doubles the game of the representation of women in a displacement that owes a great deal to the strategies of irony. Precisely because she attains complete adherence between carapace and illusion, because she vanishes as a medium and at the same time, by denying the mannequin, manages to be exactly what she seems to be – because the wig is a perfect fit for her head – Sherman clearly represents the everyday act of 'getting ready to be seen' as a form of mask; she suggests that if identity is unfixed and to some extent foreign, it is because it requires constant propping up with prostheses, with bright, borrowed, cosmetic excrescences that can no longer be considered mere accessories, however easily they can be replaced the next day.

Death Will Come and
Shall Be Wearing a Wig

More than bones gnawed by time and illness, more than the skull itself, which represents the final hour and survives us, hair is capable of mocking death. As archaeologists and tomb robbers know, there is nothing more chilling than a decrepit skeleton, worm-eaten, on the point of being reduced to dust, and the hair that accompanies it, dulled from lack of air, thin as a handful of threads, and yet in some way still brimming with a splendour and vitality that, given the conditions, is almost macabre.

Preserved in the dark night of lockets – boxes with no other music than that of memory – or spread on a pillow of a coffin (in the end, sarcophagi are simply huge lockets), hair occupies an ambiguous position between life and death, which may explain the popular idea that it continues growing on the corpse, like a parasitic plant flourishing on a broken branch.

At once a relic, a worthless trinket, an ephemeral adornment and a passport to the other world, the same strands of dead cells we comb daily are what will speak of us when we are no longer alive; like some sinister encrypted museum, hair retains the mark of our passage through life, the imponderable traces of what we were.

The mysterious Chinese mummies of Tarim, whose delicate eyelashes can still be seen, and of course their Egyptian counterparts displaying a very wide variety of hairstyles, dyes and capillary extensions (and many examples of those who, like the nobleman Maiherpri, undertook their final journey with wigs made from their own locks), all have almost silky hair that has remained intact through the centuries as if, as Alan Pauls says in his novel *Historia del pelo* (A History of Hair), 'the vital energy of the species, able to assert itself in the other world, was in fact coquetry.'

That same duality, the perturbing evasion, which, even underground, makes hair a participant in the world of the living, is perhaps what distracts us in the usual representations of death. Accustomed to the completely hairless, ironic skull, the shorn figure of *La Pelona*, we forget that hair makes its presence felt in the long goodbye with at least as much grace as fleshless bones, and that if, like any organic substance, it is subject to decay, it not only retains and radiates its elegance, but at times accompanies the skull as an artistic motif. If death traditionally wears a bony mask to announce its presence, the superimposition of a featureless face on the live skin, why should it not also appear with splendorous tresses of posthumous hair flowing in the icy wind of the afterlife?

As a support on which are draped the features, a hidden visage that blossoms after death and can be only faintly seen in outline on X-rays, the skull has not always been a funereal symbol or grim herald. In contrast to the European *danse macabre* of the fifteenth and sixteenth centuries, in which walking skeletons warn of the impermanence of all things terrestrial and censure any hint of vanity, in ancient Mexico it was a means of celebrating life, an insignia of the indestructibility of the living world. According to the art historian and publisher Paul Westheim, the fact that the

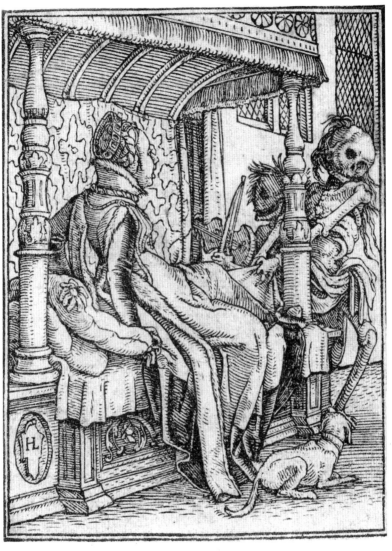

Hans Holbein the Younger, *The Duchess*, from 'The Dance of Death' series, *c.* 1526–38, woodcut depicting an entourage of dishevelled skeletons touching the feet of the duchess.

calavera, the skull, is one of the most common decorative forms in Meso-America indicates that there was nothing horrific or tragic about it; rather than being an overly mass-produced memento mori still found in everyday articles or a stark exhortation to moral reflection and penitence, it was an indisputable feature of the landscape: a familiar presence capable of integrating the end, the cessation of existence, into a more powerful cycle.

In the prints of Manuel Manilla and José Guadalupe Posada and also in celebrations of the Day of the Dead, the *calaca* (the figure of the skeleton or skull) is a friend you go out on the town with, or a beautiful woman with her well-earned wasp waist, who roars with laughter. A Mestizo figure, once shrouded in the lugubrious, admonitory colours of Christianity, she is still a symbol of death as everyday occurrence. Dressed just like any other passer-by, with a thirst for fiestas and mescal, the *calaca* is not so much a spook who jumps out unexpectedly as another guest in the household, an old acquaintance who behaves with a naturalness that allows death to be taken as a joke. It should be no surprise that she is one of the main nutrients of life but can also cause toothache – in mid-transposition of our need for carrion – in the candied form of a sugar skull.

The all-too-human face of death, who in Mexico is as likely to be seen as a bullfighter or giving herself the airs of a grand lady, has been favourable ground for displays of long hair and even revolutionary moustaches. Far from the gleaming scalps of pre-Columbian statuary, carved in obsidian or rock crystal, *La Calavera* uses hair as an ornament to avoid causing fright and so be able to pass serenely by in the light of day. The incongruence of hair that requires sebaceous glands in order to grow sprouting from bone indicates that these manifestations are wigs, flagrant hairpieces and glued-on moustaches that might or might not belong to the deceased.

And while that pileous presence might employ dresses and hats in its representations (when the flesh, what is most perishable and closest to dust, has disappeared, it seems reasonable to avail oneself of any adornment), the hair enjoys the privilege of almost post-mortem adoration thanks to its astonishing consistency, the fact that it is reminiscent of our appearance in life and is, in a way more impressive than the skull (whose recognition involves abstraction), the body itself. A head of hair is the quintessential dead body that, without fuss – although sometimes after a shudder that can involve nausea and horror – becomes a cult object, a synecdoche of the body as artifice.

Due to its inherent vanity, but above all because the very idea of ornament, the drawn-out process of 'dolling oneself up', would seem a waste of time without a sexual context (an affirmation that, ultimately, favours the propagation of life), the slightly disjointed portrayal of dishevelled death reveals that in some way the wig is to the *calaca* what the skull is to the person: a bridge, a solution to continuity capable of integrating the end into a more powerful cycle.

> A phoenix of the brain I am,
> reborn from myself,
> who as quickly as I die in one
> in another am reborn.

So writes Francisco de Quevedo in a poem which, reminiscent of Callimachus, gives voice to a wig, one of the many piles of dead hair resting on the bald heads of the living.

José Guadalupe Posada, *Profile of a Female Skeleton with a Fur Vest*, from a broadside entitled 'La Calavera de Cupido', published by Antonio Vanegas Arroyo, *c.* 1880–1910, etching on zinc.

If for want of a flourishing scalp, *La Pelona* wears a wig, an outlandish confection of dead hair, it is not only so that she can be seen in broad daylight, can conceal her intrusion into a place where she does not belong – her terrifying and in the end unconcealable otherness – but because the deceitful head of hair, glowing with life, as lissom as if it really had continued growing in the coffin, represents a triumph over finitude, a disturbingly attractive exception to a future of decomposition and rot that, among other things, allows the aptly named *Calavera Catrina* to deploy her vital impulses, with seduction being at the van.

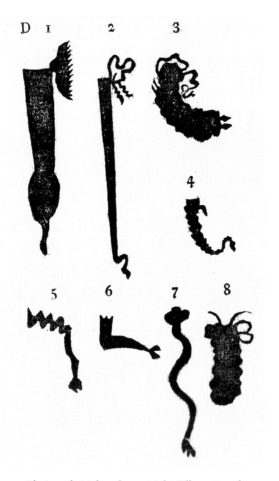

Georg Christoph Lichtenberg, *Eight Silhouettes of Student Braids*, 1783. Students' pigtails were used by Lichtenberg for his study of character. The first is close to the 'Teutonic ideal'. The seventh is an aberration not unlike a piece of hemp rope.

A Bald Wig in
Search of a Head

In a century dominated by the wig, Georg Christoph Lichtenberg discovered faces which so clearly do not belong to their owners that they run the risk of slipping off at the slightest jolt. After examining his true personality, he suggested that it would be equally valid to look from behind and infer his character from his peruke or haircut. In 1783, in reply to Johann Kaspar Lavater's *Physiognomische Fragmente* (Physiognomic Fragments), he wrote 'Fragment von Achwänzen' (Fragment on Tails), a very short, hilarious tract in which he derives the characters of three animals – pigs, dogs and humans – from nothing more than the appearance of their tails; even if, in the case of humans, the appendage in question is the pigtail of a wig.

For the intrepid observer from Göttingen, who believed that 'the most entertaining surface on earth is the human face,' the project of a capillary rhetoric that, following the laws of the renascent 'science' of physiognomy, was primarily concerned with features naturally involved satire; yet it still shook the foundations of an interpretive edifice that abused determinism and made perception its principal oracle. Two hundred years later, no lesser personage than E. H. Gombrich would return to his article to warn of the dangers of forms of art criticism that, written in language as pretentious and esoteric as Lichtenberg's parody, focus on 'expressive' qualities – the brushwork, colours and lines – as if they float in the air, unconnected to the context and ultimately to history. 'We cannot judge a face in an instant,' Lichtenberg noted, 'something must be implied by it.'

If it had not been for the rebellious wig, with its tendency to go off-kilter, we would perhaps only remember Lichtenberg as a second-rank physicist rather than the sporadic writer of insightful fragments that, even though they do not always form a whole, do make sparks without having to be rubbed together. According to Juan Villoro, who translated him into Spanish and has been sharp enough to allow his prose to be infected by the genial intelligence of the original, as a student he amused himself in the maths class by contemplating the master's lopsided wig. From the chalkboard to the hairpiece and from equations to the mysteries of fractions, the zigzagging of his attention gives a glimpse of that rare ability, honed during his life, to look through the eyes of everyday needles in a new way.

His opposition to physiognomy, the outlandish 'four-legged eagle without wings' that disturbed his sense of the rational and to which he dedicated several short treatises, was partly due to his strained, ambivalent relationship with his own body. Short and hunchbacked, the product of 'a bad draughtsman working in the dark', Lichtenberg was far from endorsing the Comte de Buffon's theory that a badly made body is capable of housing a beautiful soul, and postulated that defects can clear the path for one's own ideas.

For him, the notion of an 'anatomy of the passions', which assumed that the language of the soul can be read on the skin, was ridiculous, not so much for the distinction it makes between profound and superficial worlds manifest and latent in man, but because it resembles the theory in physics that explains the aurora borealis as the reflection of 'a swarm of herrings'. A century before Freud, he suggested that the key was to be found in dreams rather than in features. Taciturn as any good humorist, and in his later years prey to the timidity brought on by being out of synch with the times, he feared that if he advanced any further in that direction, his contemporaries would view his intuition as just one more hypothesis that took too many liberties with herrings.

Despite the difficulty of being aware of the rhetoric of one's own era, that blindness that impedes us from perceiving the peculiarities of the present for lack of an effective point of comparison, of a contrast that puts the singularity of our customs into perspective, he was capable of criticizing such contemporary institutions as belief in God and corsets. With his restless, ironic eye and mastery of droll analogy, Lichtenberg demonstrated that the most diverse of superstitions are in some way related. The problem of corsets was not only their oppressive function and deleterious effects on female health, but their tendency to repress and narrow the European mind. That observation was so penetrating and subversive that the scrawny misanthrope did not dare develop it outside his *sudelbücher,* his now famous accounting scrapbooks, and entrusted their publication to a friend. A defender of *sapere aude,* he was aware that the torch of truth would singe some wigs and not a few beards; rather than a confrontational writer, he was an amateur visionary who wrote scrawled notes to himself, unclassifiable notes that, while contradictory, have reached out to the future.

Thanks to Lavater's discovery of and emphasis on the face, his imitators were tireless in their praise of the wig, and even master wigmakers saw the interpretive fever as a new commercial line for their products. Although it is not easy to reflect objectively on a sort of rug worn on the head until death, Lichtenberg, who owed the turn taken in his career to it, was incapable of omitting from his hazardous research that powdered, hirsute convention, in itself as fatuous and obsolescent as the corset. If he did not go so far as to consider whether free thought is compatible with a somewhat rancid, outdated gizmo that makes no attempt to hide its aristocratic lineage and is a symbol of hierarchy and power (Lichtenberg witnessed the fury of the French Revolution, with its rage for shaving off crowns and privileges with the razor of the guillotine), he did not hesitate to approach the wig with the awed caution of someone visiting an improbable country, an astonishing floating island of hair on which one could fantasize about a novel that will never be written.

Although nothing would have delighted him so much as to contribute to the design and overall plan in the case that he was reborn, Lichtenberg thanked the heavens that the transformation of bodies was confined to the superficial. If rather than a simple cosmetic aid, we had, for example, the power of assemblage, then all and sundry would make themselves into headstrong monsters, theorizing scarecrows with extensions and prostheses, set in motion by distorted self-images. But even as the material for a deficient, limited, do-it-yourself project, the body is constantly manipulated in the quest for personal affirmation, for an incarnation of the I that both adheres to and reflects desires. Men do not personally inhabit the world, suggested the 'Colon of Hypochondria'; in their place they send a doll that they dress up as they please.

However much appearance might have become the sum of detachable parts, in a somewhat capricious self-proclamation always involving coercion, it came up against frontiers that were difficult to cross, against the fashionable notion of the body as a touchstone, irrevocable matter. That limiting factor could, nevertheless, be seen as an advantage. Despite hours spent on personal grooming, the incipient control on how we look permits a focus on self-invention along other, less fickle lines, beyond what the mirror might be capable of reflecting. Rather than an affected, stiff obstacle, for Lichtenberg the wig was that consensual expedient for both complying with social norms and being able to dedicate oneself to thought.

A guardian of the frontier of the public and private worlds, instead of joining the Romantic Movement and denying the bonds and atavisms associated with hairstyling, Lichtenberg kept faith with the wig, a strange loyalty for a declared Francophobe. In spite of the fact that few people knew as well as he that fashion is not limited to apparel or the need to dazzle others, the pressure exerted by the wig on his parietal bones was no obstacle to bewigged thought, respectful of convention and rigid as a mask. In fact, he was doing nothing more than conforming to the uniform of the Enlightenment philosopher: his wig was almost identical to, possibly even the same size as, his beloved Kant's. With an eye to the cliché that the face is the mirror of the soul, he noted that if philosophers had a dressing table sufficiently vast to see their whole selves reflected, they, along with the frivolous and vain, would never move away from it.

With all the contradictions of the person who renounces a system, the great tightrope walker of the imbalances between the mind and body managed to form opinions on the most unthought-of matters thanks to an ability to provide his doll, his representative in the world, with the safe conduct of a white

Matthew Darly, *Tight Lacing or Hold Fast Behind*, 1777, hand-coloured etching and engraving.

wig, and so cease to concern himself with the choreography of the social dance. As with Leibniz before him, he understood the importance of facade, the representation that does not attack established sentiments; a facade that, since it in some way reflects our needs and appetites, he would come to believe in. 'Man is ultimately so free a being that his right to *be* what he believes himself to be cannot be contested.'

In and Out of the Theatre

'So may the outward shows be least themselves: The world is still deceived with ornament,' wrote William Shakespeare in *The Merchant of Venice* (Act III, Scene 2). Far from fading into the air of a masonry stage, amid actors speaking in sparkling verse, many of them wearing wigs and theoretically period costume, those words benefit from the distance imposed by the dramatic genre and touch a sore spot due to the fact that they are pronounced outside the world, in an artificial sphere, that miniature globe capable of reflecting and encompassing the world.

Totus mundus agit histrionem (literally, all the world plays a role) was the inscription to be read above the entrance to the Globe Theatre in London. But if Bassanio's voice were not projected and his gestures not rehearsed over and over until they attained the naturalness of artifice, perhaps his lament regarding deception and the dangers hidden behind the veil of appearance would pass unnoticed, as are so many things said daily on the other side of 'the fourth wall', in the wide social field of the visible, where we are all truly actors.

As a part of his distrust of the promises of ornament, the slippery gap between splendour and reality, the Shakespearean character also lashes out at the sorcery of the wig:

So are those crisped snaky golden locks
Which make such wanton gambols with the wind,
Upon supposed fairness, often known
To be the dowry of a second head,
The skull that bred them in the sepulchre.

According to the humble Venetian, who, because of his friend Antonio, has been forced to pledge a pound of human flesh in order to gain the rich heiress Portia, the borrowed beauty of the wig, its locks stolen from the grave, is simply a postponement of disillusion, a dismal tribute to nothing, to what has no place and will soon show the seams of its own failure.

In the style of the set of Chinese boxes in *Hamlet* – in which the characters attend a function scarcely different to the tragedy they themselves play out, and in which the truth will be unveiled – the condemnation of the theatre of life acquires greater force when spoken from the stage. The realm of appearance that cosmetics and wigs perpetuate and rarely combat, that vast dance of errors and hypocrisy in which each person does his utmost to pretend and present himself as someone else, can perhaps only be effectively censured from the sphere of dramatic representation, where artificiality is complete and, paradoxically, more convincing, more alive.

Shylock, the Jewish moneylender in *The Merchant of Venice*, has traditionally been played wearing a red wig and with a large, hooked nose. Although there is not the least indication in the text as to his appearance, the character has survived over three or four centuries thanks to that wig and outsized nose; it is by virtue of the unnaturalness of his well-known mask, the stereotype it gives body and voice to (person comes from *per sonare*, to speak through), that, as a caricature of avarice, someone as intransigent as Shylock is capable of inspiring pity. Shakespeare makes use of the mental cliché guaranteed by the wig to subvert expectations and generate sympathy for a deceptively secondary character, no more unhinged by wealth than his Catholic peers.

While Bassanio's distrust of glitter and simulation could also include Shylock's wig (that garish hairpiece we have all seen smouldering on the stage), his speech unfolds on the hierarchical plane of representation, inside that small Chinese box in which time can stop or make leaps, and where the wig is not merely a false, hirsute accessory but the entrails of the individual made visible. Untouched by Bassanio's suspicion, it is in fact through the wig – and the large-nosed mask, the ventriloquist's voice in which the actor is made to speak – that his censure succeeds in ruffling the hairpieces and toupees of the planet.

Although in their historical origins, wigs and masks coexisted in primitive hunting rites or as instruments of supernatural power and invocations, the wig had a parallel life outside those ritual spaces, on the margins of the exceptional periods of trance and sacred celebration. Setting aside theatre, a ritual that does not wait for the cyclical recurrence of the seasons to repeat itself, the mask is to be found during Carnival and such annual ceremonies and festivities as Halloween. In contrast, the wig is present every day, so profane and earthly that it is still a symbol of vanity, so ostentatious and possibly out of place that it is still plagued by accusations of fraud, of being a superficial and narcissistic adornment, a pitiful swindle.

In classical antiquity, when the observance of ritual was inseparable from political life, there were obligatory periods of abstinence that culminated in propitiatory celebrations steeped in

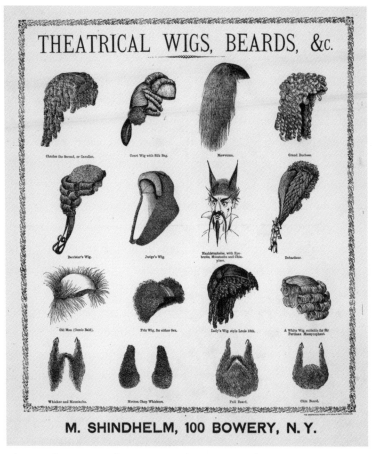

Theatrical Wigs, Beards, &c., 1870 advertisement for costume wigs and beards manufactured by Michael Shindhelm for use in theatrical productions.

dancing, wine and music. Dressed in the skins of goats and other animals, and after having 'let their hair down', women would give themselves up to erotic flagellation, ritual copulation and a wide variety of esoteric sacrifices. The noisiest rituals were the bacchanals, where the retinue of dishevelled women celebrating a new epiphany of Dionysus allowed themselves to be transported by the sense of liberation transmitted by the god of masks; they uttered euphoric cries and danced wildly, drank wine, milk and potions that seemed to spring spontaneously from the earth, and were caught up in a frenzy, a mania not even they could explain. According to Walter Otto, a scholar of the Dionysian myth, the sudden appearance of the deranged god brought about a transformation in which inebriation and delirium were mixed with arousal and the urge for annihilation, to the extent that many women felt the desire to allow wild beasts to feed from their breasts. In a mockery of the established order and norms, the thunder of the bacchantes carried with it everything that crossed their path, as if in the blink of an eye the floodgates holding back the contagious torrent of life had opened. But sooner or later the period of licentiousness and rapture came to an end, the masks and animal skins were stowed away until the next festival, but wigs, significantly, remained outside the closet.

(In relation to these rites, in Euripides' powerful play *The Bacchae* the wig plays a central role in both the development of the piece and the staging. Seduced by the irrational idea of uncovering the mystery cults to which men are not admitted, Pentheus, the king of Thebes, succumbs to the temptation of cross-dressing as a means of achieving his sacrilegious act of voyeurism. The primary element of his disguise – more important than the *peplos* (women's dress) or even the thyrsus that acts as a safe conduct – is a blond hairpiece, long locks of ruffled curls. When, at Dionysus' instigation, the Maenads pull Pentheus down from the tree where he is spying on them, he removes his wig so that he will be recognized, at least by his mother Agave, who is at the head of the furious pack; despite this act of self-revelation, Pentheus' limbs are unceremoniously torn off.

In terms of the staging, Jan Kott points out that the trajectory of the long, blond, curly wig must be one of the most brilliant uses of a prop in the whole history of theatre. Disdainful of drunken cults and sceptical of Dionysus' divinity, Pentheus stripped him of the curled, scented hairpiece he had worn on his arrival in Thebes so as to pass as a stranger; then that same wig is used for the conversion of Pentheus into a propitiatory victim and his leonine head into a hunting trophy exhibited on the thyrsus. In this way Dionysus, the god of masks and metamorphosis who, according to Nietzsche's controversial interpretation, was the originary hero of all Greek tragedies – in this interpretation Oedipus and Prometheus are just his avatars – merits the right to be also considered the god of wigs.)

Due to the etymological thread connecting it to personality, one could say that, to a greater extent than all the successors to a head of hair, everyday life is swamped with masks: masks for the social roles we play, masks for hiding behind in the presence of others, masks for achieving the elusive I we would like to be, masks in which to confront the mirror . . . but the wig, in contrast to protean cuticle that could be mistaken for the epidermis, is effectively among us, superimposed on the natural hair (or its lack) in all its caressing materiality, displacing or supplanting it in an operation devoid of sanctity and often of glamour.

An individual who appears in public wearing a hairpiece knows that others will scrutinize him and seek to establish just how far 'things are as they seem'; but whether it is a temporary joke or a particular party piece, the wig is not an element of the costume, a pretext for a wearyingly long role-play, but a continuation of the body, a restitution of youth, 'no less subjectively gratifying for being objectively illusory', according to Salvador

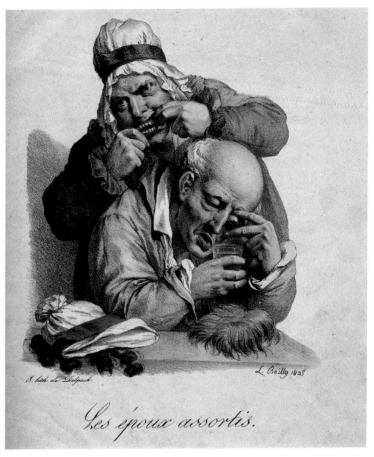

Les époux assortis.

Louis Boilly, *The Matched Pair*, 1825, colour lithograph by Delpech
depicting a couple assembling their false body parts: false teeth,
a glass eye and wigs.

Novo; a recently obtained crowning glory for exhibiting and
projecting oneself better in public, with more aplomb and, if
the word does not seem too exaggerated, greater 'naturalness'.

Louis XIV, on imposing the reign of the wig after having
disdained it in his youth, was never again seen without one,
except in the presence of his hairdresser M. Binet, and in his

bedchamber the pages had to carry out their tasks behind a complex series of curtains. Rather than the embarrassment of being seen naked, what appears to have been at stake here is lack, the indignity of being incomplete, that understandable unwillingness to reveal what is all-too-well known but, even so, should not be uncovered.

As a detachable object, because it can be lost or substituted, because it completes a drive that goes beyond the cosmetic, the wig is a form of psychological prosthesis; the person wearing one is capable of becoming someone else, an analogy of himself behind which, to some extent, he hides, but in which he is also vindicated. And, as with any prosthesis, one should perhaps wait a few days before fully integrating it into one's sense of self in order to become accustomed to its volume, that numbness when the touch of fingertips does not trigger an electrical signal, but above all to reconcile oneself to the new way one is perceived and deciphered by others.

Wigs, toupees and extensions that pile up in lost property offices cannot be compared with leftover theatre props or the cast-offs of some possibly fortunate disguise; those orphan hairs, those strange aerial rugs left on the seat of a train, are not, or not always, as Shakespeare described ornament, 'the guiled shore to a most dangerous sea', but authentic accidental amputations, orthopaedic losses comparable to the loss of an artificial arm made from flesh and bone, with genuine muscles and tendons, or of a mask that, like the ones worn by the Aztecs for sacrifices, is made from human skin.

Stony Hair

I f for Plato the body is a shadow, the hateful marrow opposed to the excellence of death, hair can be nothing more than the shadow of a shadow, a contemptible and ridiculous accessory of that clothing we must leave behind at the end of our life on Earth. In *Parmenides*, through the thoughts of the young Socrates, we learn that there cannot be a separate Idea of hair, just as there cannot be one of dirt. Hair, as an example of something unimportant and grotesque in which perfection has no place, is on the margins of thought, along with mud.

Not all the Greeks shared that disdain for the human body. It was the object of care, embellishment and aesthetic exaltation, and perhaps as a nation it would be more appropriate to describe it using a word invented by Plato: in contrast to the philosopher, at permanent war with the body and hoping to learn how to annihilate it, was his friend, *filosomate* (lover of all bodies).

Artists were not slow in transplanting the human body into their representations of the gods. Although Aphrodite has something of every woman, during the splendorous age of Greek art she had the body of one woman: Phryne, the hetaira who won a legal case with no other argument than her beauty. Praxiteles, who shared with Parrhasius the intrepidity or insolence of lending the gods the bodies of the prostitutes they loved, used her as the model for the first life-sized, female nude sculpture. In relation to its replica in gold, which stood on a column of Pantelic marble in Delphi, the Cynic Crates said that it was a monument to the incontinence of the Greeks.

Given that it was less than a shadow, in that epoch hair received an astonishing amount of attention, and in Athens there was even a tribunal that fined citizens who neglected it. In contrast to his idealistic contemporaries, Praxiteles was deeply interested in it. The statues ascribed to him display amazing sensuality and grace; their undulating coiffures possess a fluidity that seems to deny their marble origin. In the Aphrodite inspired by Phryne, where one clearly sees why she is the goddess of sexuality and reproduction, there is something serpentine and hypnotic about the hair. As if conscious of the Medusa effect, she wears it tied at the nape of the neck. Rather than the implacable blindness of her eyes, it is the sleeping curls of the snake, just one step from awakening to life, that petrify us to the point of changing places with the statue.

It has been noted that Praxiteles and other artists sculpted the mount of Venus completely smooth. Instead of being a faithful representation of contemporary hair-removal practices, one could say that his statuary shaving was an attempt to produce a certain coldness and distance. It is also quite likely that pubic hair was left to the charge of the painter who completed the pieces; while the strident whiteness of Greek ruins might make one suppose otherwise, they were all coloured. Those same pubic regions that no one is sure whether or not to touch – the statues are provocative, there is a hint of the Galatea about them – would later be censored by the application of vines and biblical fig leaves: during the Renaissance there was a flourishing professional guild known as the *braghettoni*, composed of artists of the private parts whose task it was to naturalistically cover those disturbing deltas.

Plato, who did not hold images in high esteem and was, in his way, an iconoclast, denounced the painters and sculptors of his time for producing so many errant images. Despite the fact that many of those sculptors were, like Parrhasius, seeking to capture the moral expression of the soul at the decisive moment, he stigmatized them as sophists of the visible world. Reproducing in great detail the perishable waste of the transitory dungeon of the body and, to a greater extent, the filth of hair, involved using the darkness of the human cave to give pleasure, a dishonest mode of amusement that distances us from the imperturbable splendour of Forms (particularly when involving the wig, for which the term *phenake*, meaning 'false hair', is employed). Long before Occam took his famous razor to Plato's metaphysical beard, the latter had already shaved the dross and excrescences, the disorienting tangle of the sensible world.

Through a somewhat incongruous or audacious trick of fate, it is thanks to marble, the stone of immutability, that we have knowledge of the fashions of those times. Set in the best blocks from Naxos and Paros is the whole range of the hairstyles of antiquity, its braids and diadems. The image of Plato himself, with that thick beard and the stern fringe, has come to us thanks to the marmoreal art, an art that, *sub specie hominis*, composes our imitation of immortality.

Wigs also achieved the status of a *grand cru* of stone. In Egypt, the Great Sphinx of Giza, whose features have been softened by time, is crowned by an imposing pharaonic wig sculpted on a small mountain of limestone. Beyond her enduring enigma and the sometimes idiotic hypotheses about the missing nose, it is a surprise to find in this figure the monumental representation of a hairpiece that, as far as is known, was accompanied by a straight, jutting beard, also superimposed.

In spite of the fact that only through parody can we imagine a dialogue in which the Idea separated from the wig is debated – Aristippus, the philosopher of pleasure, might have provoked his former master Socrates by such insolence – sculptors of every era have had no problems with chiselling hairpieces as haloes of beauty and have even dared to carve the odd detachable wig, although it is uncertain if this was done to enhance the mimesis or so that the hairpiece could be substituted in accordance with the already insistent if rather vague cry of fashion. From Praxiteles to the abundance of Renaissance busts, hair has been an occasion to display virtuosity of technique; in the end, despite the gravitas of stone, sculptural art invites closeness, a circling of the represented body accompanied by a simultaneous appreciation of the artifice.

In terms of the statuary of Rome, where wigs caused such a furore that virgin hair had to be imported from India and Germany, it is possible to find examples of false heads of marble hair as daring as they are discordant. There are statues in which the contrast between self and other in fact seems to be the theme of the work, and others in which the tresses were artfully added later – as is perhaps characteristic of the wig – to enliven the bust of some unknown person and increase its value. In *The Book of Perfumes* (1865), Eugène Rimmel, the erudite innovator of cosmetics, mentions wigs of a variety of colours, made of quarried marble from all around the world, that served as accessories to the bust of Julia Semiamira, the mother of Heliogabalus, and which 'could be removed at pleasure'. There are also

Portrait Head of Julia Titi, marble Roman sculpture, *c.* AD 90.
This popular hairstyle utilized hair extensions and dramatic
curls piled high in a proto-Marie-Antoinette style.

marbles of Julia Domna and Fulvia Plautilla (mother and wife
of the emperor Caracalla, respectively) that are practically model
kits, although it is not clear if their detachable hairpieces reflected
contemporary practice (it was considered a sign of good breeding to wear a wig on the kalends of January) or were just a
labour-saving exercise on the part of the sculptor.

All attempts to defy time involve a degree of desperation,
but it may be that those empresses understood the horror of

Bust of Julia Domna (empress consort), marble Roman sculpture, late 2nd century AD–early 3rd century AD. A pair of curls peep out from under the wig.

seeing themselves petrified, ever more distant in their marble portrayals and so, unlike Dorian Gray, stipulated that their sculptures be changeable devices that faithfully accompanied them and could be modified as they aged.

Nowadays, no one questions the appropriateness of capturing the body – that fleeting shadow – in a particular instant. Only familiarity, the imperceptible persuasion of habit, explains how the ideal of beauty has assimilated the notion that marble – nothing more than humble clay – is petrified flesh, at once the image and refutation of mutable appearance.

Imagine the astonishment if, in some reverse form of the sculptural operation, an inevitably leaky container was made – in the case of Meret Oppenheim, it would be a coffee cup – from nothing more than hair.

Wigs at the Extremes of Crime

The wig has always been part of the stage make-up of criminals. For decades the south of France was hounded by a team of bank robbers known as the *Gang des postiches* (Wigs Gang) and, in bygone days, highwaymen pretending to be down-at-heel nobles wore exuberant stolen hairpieces when almost literally fleecing travellers. The term 'fleecing' is both suggestive and pertinent: it indicates that there is no limit to what can be stripped bare. But there was a time when wigs were so highly valued that they became one of the prime targets of the criminal classes. A scene from a comedy of errors: in a dark, deserted forest, hooded bandits wearing false hair but with their faces uncovered – some possibly dressed as women – lay a trap for other similarly bedecked men in order to make off with their wigs.

As an old ploy of the criminal world, cross-dressing is not simply an element of camouflage; the parallel personality involved in disguise encourages daring: wrapped in otherness, outside himself due to the conjuring tricks of the toilette and simple costume changes, the assailant carries out his misdeeds under the fearless misconception that crime and punishment are no concern of his. That disjunction, which cannot be put down to mere cosmetic effect, frequently appears in sexual attacks, where the fracture of identity can range from the unlikely and short-lived to the profound disorder of psychosis: in a risible version of the doctor played by Michael Caine in *Dressed to Kill*, where a change of costume allows the character to express his repressed personality – the vengeful alter ego Bobbi, a cross-dressing version of Jack the Ripper – in the Mexico City metro a certain individual once donned a wig and female clothing to sexually assault women in the rush-hour crush (the newspapers had a field day: 'Dressed to Grope').

Jacques Mesrine, France's public enemy number one in the 1970s, better known as Monsieur-tout-le-monde (Mr Everybody), was a transformation artist guided by the precepts of the economy of disguise. At the height of his career as an assailant, kidnapper and bank robber he only had to change his wig and glasses to throw police departments off the scent. As if capable of voluntarily divesting himself of his undeniable charisma, when on his way to a new heist, the role of the toupeed office-worker allowed him to keep a cool head. He perhaps counted on the consequent commiseration and mild embarrassment increasing the surprise factor.

Although detectives imitate and perfect the wiles of their prey, it is unusual for wigs to predominate in the office furnishings of police departments. In the mid-eighteenth century, however, Antoine de Sartine, one of the most powerful men in France, Lieutenant General of Police of Paris and reputedly a master of vigilance and espionage, had a marked weakness for wigs, particularly those rich in curls, and amassed a significant collection of the most expensive models.

According to dreamy psychologists, often under the influence of an idée fixe, the passion for collecting is rooted in some form of sexual disorder. Sartine did not accumulate wigs – or not

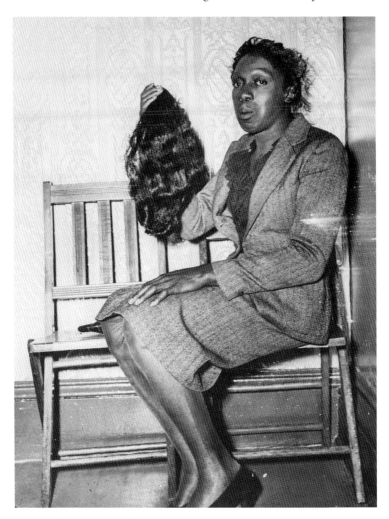

Weegee (Arthur H. Fellig), *Transvestite Robber/A Thief Dressed as a Woman*, 1945, gelatin silver, printed later.

exclusively – for morbid contemplation or the sedentary pastime of caressing their unnatural fibres. In charge of maintaining not only law and order, but public health, hygiene and even the cleaning and lighting of the city, the implacable lieutenant general

Some of the many faces of Jacques Mesrine. Photo-booth self-portraits, 1978.

used his eighty wigs to dress as the occasion demanded. Roland Barthes, in his text on the Marquis de Sade (an almost lifelong victim of Sartine's vigilance), lingers on that contradictory figure, noting that he had a special wig for interrogations known as the *inexorable,* a form of 'snake headdress', and another for good luck, from which hung five long ringlets. The powdered model he wore for portraits (one of which presided over every police station in Paris) was soon christened with his name and was adopted by a growing number of magistrates, both within France and beyond, as a symbol of impartiality and justice. The wig, so often persecuted and besieged, in this way passed to the side of the persecutors.

Barthes classifies this excessive interest in hairy trifles as a 'psychopathological condition'. If the society had been more just, he suggests, Sartine would have been imprisoned for monomania, for follicular fetishism, or at least kept under close observation by his officers. He had become famous throughout Europe for the extent of the tentacles of his secret police; their methods were not exactly legal, but they were productive, with the confiscation of correspondence a speciality. In the search for compromising clues or juicy declarations, even ordinary citizens were included in their snooping, and after broadening their sources of information through interrogations and paid denunciations in houses of prostitution and bordellos, confessionals and convents, one of their missions was to give the king daily reports on the habits and sexual exploits of everyone in Versailles and Paris. The ageing Louis XV and his official mistress, Madame de Pompadour, had not had carnal knowledge of one another for over a decade, but they got enormous enjoyment from the spicy summaries that, under the pretext of curbing licentiousness and depravity, exposed the strangest behaviours and libidinal excesses of the French nation.

Gossip as a priceless pleasure of the royalty had a great deal to do with the fact that the Marquis de Sade was constantly in and out of prison and condemned to a life of strict vigilance. While his immediate persecutor was Inspector Louis Marais, the outstanding authority on licentiousness, the 'Divine Marquis' developed an unbounded hatred of Marais's superior, knowing him to be responsible for the cruel attention given to his blasphemy, his sporadic excesses and brief transgressions in the bedchamber. With the at times diabolical brilliance of his pen – a *plume* that grew taller with each year spent behind bars, as if it were capable of gathering momentum from monotony and repetition – Sade made a sketch of Sartine's character that portrayed the lieutenant general of police and later director, and censor, of the Royal Library as the real degenerate, the reprobate society had to be protected from. He described him as having 'issued forth from the left side of Father Torquemada' and called him 'the most politically corrupt and consummately depraved wretch ever to light up the sky'.

Also a book collector, Sartine – who deserved to pass into the annals of history as 'the man of a thousand wigs' – may well have donned a special wig to read with unhealthy delight the titles to be included on the prohibited list, and it is not impossible that he had a favourite one for writing the reports in which, with the manic meticulousness of a person who understands the importance of detail for the police, he exposed the debauched behaviour and elaborate orgies of his contemporaries.

History offers other examples of wig collections. In *The Strange Life of Objects*, the painstaking collector of collectors Maurice Rheims notes the case of the Duke of Portland who,

Romina Power in *Marquis de Sade: Justine* (1969), directed by Jesús Franco.

Erich von Götha, illustration in *Journal de Sartine* (2007).

in the late nineteenth century, used to go out in disguise to take the train in search of additions to his cabinet of capillary curiosities. And one could hardly forget the collection of almost a thousand owned by Louis XIV, who might also be said to have collected master wigmakers: he had no fewer than forty in his service. But it is possible that none of these achieves the majesty and diversity, in the fullest sense of the roles that an actor might play in the theatre, of the collection belonging to the omniscient, versatile Sartine, who first transformed himself from a snoop and inspector into a bibliophile, then into Secretary of State for the Navy, only later, during the Reign of Terror, to elude the guillotine by a hair's breadth and return to Barcelona, the city of his birth, under the alias of Señor Sardina and the mask of a mild-mannered, retired Enlightenment gentleman of letters.

Although Sade did not begin to write his novels of deviancy and perversion until after Sartine had left office, it is tempting to compare the ways in which, from opposing sides of the walls of the Bastille, they made outrageous sexual activity into a subject for writing.

The Marquis, possibly still wearing the courtly wig of his youth, lingered on dry descriptions of the coupling of bodies in all the variants his truculent imagination dictated, and with a distance that owes much to aloofness and ennui, perhaps inspired by the strict prison rules, enumerated the mechanical movements of humiliation and torture involving both pleasure and pain to offer an unvarnished, almost bureaucratic report of the abuses of the flesh and pornographic brutality (as if rather than a contribution to erotic literature, a toned-up version of Choderlos de Laclos' *Liaisons dangereuses*, his project consisted of composing a grand encyclopaedia of sexual atrocity, a titanic, perhaps edifying in some nauseating way, classification of the throwaway pleasures of the body and the diverse aberrations humans are capable of when their fantasies are triggered by a taste for profanation and blasphemy). By contrast, Sartine, still in the stunning, propitiatory wig he wore for lewd denunciations, for impassioned accusation, sat down to write up police reports on stark intimacy, classified documents that, due to the convolutions of excessive power, had the primary intention of titillating the royal couple, of reviving their dwindling sexual appetites, and amused himself recompiling his subalterns' logbooks to recreate, down to the last split hair, the most depraved proposals, the most outlandish, immoral postures, the snares and betrayals that encourage scandal, as if his eager network of informants and bloodhounds were committed not to the enforcement of public order but the strange task of stimulating the erotic imagination.

On Nudity; or, Venus in a Wig

I t was Sacher-Masoch who first noted the incongruity of a marble statue dressed in furs. Through a subtle maud-itism and a degree of post-romantic naivety, the image, inspired by Titian (which anticipated that no less irresistible one of a woman of haughty beauty and an ice-cold air, naked beneath a sable coat), sparks fantasies of the cave-dwelling variety in which the iciness of a delicate body, scantily clad in the cast-offs of the hunt, is about to succumb to a sensual experience.

In absolute contrast to Sacher-Masoch's Venus in Furs is the doll-fetish Oskar Kokoschka had made in an attack of pique when he discovered that his lover, Alma Mahler, had left him for someone else. The life-size replica, work of the unsuccessful artist Hermine Moos, reproduced the feel of human skin by means of a sort of mesh of tiny white feathers that, to the paint-er's dissatisfaction, horribly disrupted the illusion of the simulacrum and cooled the ardour of any attempt to dress the doll by reminding him – as he said – of the pelt of a polar bear.

Anticlimactic upholstery rather than an obedient Eve sub-stitute, a piece of proto-surrealism reminiscent of Meret Oppenheim's objects, the 'infamous doll' was a parody of woman dressed in plush. In spite of her childlike air, and perhaps pre-cisely because she lacked the rubber and silicon of present-day sex machines, the object had an unmistakably feminine charm thanks in part to its thick auburn hair and the fact that, following Kokoschka's precise instructions, she was able to close her eyes. As some form of consolation, the spurned lover was at least able to sink his fingers into those silken tresses and respond to the mendacious wink of the empty eyes.

'The Silent Woman', as the painter used to introduce her, obviously lacked the impetuous soul of Alma Mahler – although not her striking eyebrows – but withstood long sessions as an improbably furry mannequin. Converted into a model but never a wife, she allowed herself to be dressed and undressed during sexually charged ceremonies in which the use of clothing to hide the white fuzz in some way reinvented her nudity. In contrast to a dominatrix who, clad in leather and furs, seems ready to flay her partners, the doll – a dispassionate Venus, a compensation for failed love – became the victim of the sadistic urges of her owner, who on a debauched night of divorce and burial, bathed in the ritual blood of wine, beheaded her.

At the opposite extremes of the sense of touch, the Venus in furs and Kokoschka's feathered doll reflect the fact that human nudity directly implies a covering, a borrowed skin, the surreptitious or tactile presence of hair. In contrast to the mere absence of clothing, rather than a limiting state or condition, nudity carries with it the act of denuding, whether voluntary or unforeseen. It is so relative, or passing, or never fully completed, that in the charged, one might even say interminable, process of taking off one garment after another even the skin – the top rung on the ladder of the striptease – seems to be concealing something, to be setting itself between the voracity of the eye and desire.

Nudity, particularly if it involves animal skins, takes us back to our origins, to the stage of human evolution when the practice

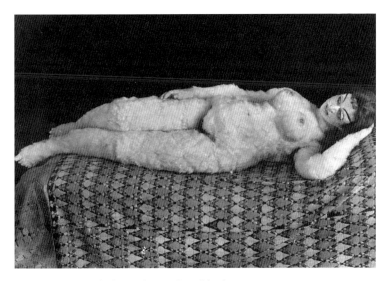

Plush Venus, made for Oskar Kokoschka by Henriette Moos in 1919.

of wearing another's plumage ran in parallel to the loss of body
hair, until the vulnerable, tremulous appearance we all now
know was reached, a state comparable to goose flesh, which,
with good reason, led the Greeks to come up with the ridiculous
term 'featherless biped'.* The invention of clothing as part of
the courting ritual, as a theatrical prop that exaggerates and
complicates the display of the body, led to the gradual disappearance of our hairy armour plating. The human epidermis,
with its random scattering of attractively hirsute islands –
mammalian blotches, each seductive in its own way – whether
the result of early culture or that second nature of skin which,

---

* In relation to origins, in Genesis 3:21, God gives the first humans
garments of animal skins as a substitute for the improvised fig leaves.
The absence of clothing, unnoticed until the act of disobedience, would
from then on signify the shameful perception of the body and symbols
of sexuality; a literal, stark discovery of what in Paradise was cloaked in
grace, 'dressed' in the glory of God.

through eye-catching artifice and effects that strengthen the magnetic fields of bodies, would soon display thermal qualities.

Once the dyad of covering and nudity formed part of the experience of the body, vast areas covered in hair were downgraded and concealed beneath fabrics, like some strange, convoluted variety of the obscene: not only pubic hair and the bushy growths of the axillae, but the hair of our heads – usually placed in a separate category – have been the object of strict concealment and observation. It is possibly because the act of unloosing one's hair is just one step from undoing one's buttons that nuns wore wimples to underscore their exclusive devotion to Christ, while when orthodox Jewish women marry they cut their hair short and shield it from view by means of a sort of modesty wig – a *sheitel* – for which, naturally, there is a kosher certification. (The heavy veils and burkas worn by many Arab women also participate in the battle against the enchantment of hair, but in doing so take in the whole face.)

In spite of the fact that, if grown long enough, hair can be a form of clothing – think of Mary Magdalene or Lady Godiva – its luxuriance and disorder suggest nakedness. As with Kokoschka's sacrificial doll – the incarnation of sexual availability – Sacher-Masoch's simultaneously primitive and clinical, futuristic and cruel goddess wears her loose hair in thick, reddish curls that, over and above the contrast with her despotic beauty, proclaim that when she covers herself in skins she is in fact nude.

Although the wig might be considered a garment (from a certain point of view, not so different from the passion-killing nightcap), and one of its functions is to conceal cranial deforestation, it is not necessarily on the side of apparel. In some form of continuation of the voluptuousness of touch suggested by Sacher-Masoch, the designer Martin Margiela had the audacity to unite the fascination of furs with the attraction of hair. In addition to leaving chinchillas and pine martens in peace, his wig coats relocate the sensual call of hair to make it into a new, figure-hugging wrap. On his catwalks, nearly naked models – authentic Venuses of the wig – wear jackets made from synthetic hair that, like surrealist miniskirts, endow the body with a feline aura, with an impossibly elusive quality.

Like lace or veils, like carnival masks or even fans, the wig – even in the exceptional form of a jacket – has the effect of uncovering the body, exalting it rather than simply dressing it; thanks to the addition of a layer, the body insinuates itself and displays and declares its loss of innocence: it succeeds in awakening in others the mental processes of eager desire.

Wig jacket creations by Belgian fashion designer Martin Margiela as displayed at Palais Galliera fashion museum in Paris, 2018.

It is said Louis-François-Armand de Vignerot du Plessis, 3rd Duke of Richelieu, whose name is associated with the invention of mayonnaise, used to hold exclusive banquets where the guests were not allowed to wear any clothing. Apparently his invitees had no problem in respecting this unusual form of etiquette, but did turn up punctually in their wigs, without which, rather than naked, they perhaps felt uncomfortable and out of place – if not imposters; as if in addition to giving up their clothes they had been obliged to temporarily change their faces.

Far from the gall of pornographic exhibition or the vulnerability of a person forced to undress, there are forms of nudity achieved through the complicity of clothing and the imagination, by means of paradoxical garments that conceal, blur or delay, but which, just for those reasons, reveal all.

If the sensuality of female hair allows a striptease to include, at one of its most decisive moments, the removal of the veil (the coif or the *sheitel*), it also shows that the act begins with the choice of a propitiatory wig that, as soon as its assurance seeps into the bearer, does not even need to be removed.

Reinvention by Hair

The desire to display a blond mane, that peroxide phantasm to be found in both the *Iliad* and advertisements, is perhaps less decisive than the idea of transforming oneself by means of hair. If the golden ideal represented by Aphrodite was capable of triggering the earliest essays into dyeing and simulation (some of them so experimental that they ended by devastating the cranial vegetation), the possibility of reinventing oneself by a chromatic blaze, the miraculous whim of straightening in a few short hours what nature had curled, of concealing grey hairs with proto-punk hues that include lilac and violet, goes much further than being a weapon of mass seduction: it is the shameless defence of artifice, a celebration of the plasticity of the body – already applauded, with certain reservations, by Ovid in *The Art of Love* – which a woman uses to take control of her appearance.

Johannes Agricola's puritan admonition that a woman knows no greater pleasure than arranging her hair seems little in comparison with the joy of consummating in a single sitting the

Constance Towers in *The Naked Kiss* (1964), directed by Samuel Fuller. Her character, Kelly, makes hair an accomplice in every rite of passage. Having shorn her head after a betrayal, and wearing a wig while working as a prostitute, she only allows her hair to grow again when she attempts to change her life.

metamorphosis of the self, its reconfiguration by simply pouring a potion over one's head. The so-called medicinal plants or tinctures of *Iris germanica*, at one time the marks of prostitution, have been the accomplices of the liberated woman since Roman times, when the risks of getting involved in the oldest profession – that ambiguity embodied by Messalina and which gave so much grist for the mills of satirical poets – or of ending up with straw when you wanted corn seemed much less serious in comparison with the satisfaction of trying out an über-blond look, the euphoria of achieving an *ad libitum* Carnival, of turning one's back on nature to refresh one's charms.

Over and above the simple wiles of make-up, it is a conscious alteration of the way in which we present ourselves to the world, a break with the past and move towards fantasy and temptation, towards a form of beauty that was never before on the scene and which consists of appropriating the body, exploring its malleability, re-encountering the person one still has to become – even if the results are out of this world. After all, according to Baudelaire, the profound spirituality of the toilette is not only a response to a disgust by the real; it shares a desire for self-expression in which that aesthetic of individualism the dandies took to extremes plays a role, an aesthetic charged with rebellion and irreverence but also with the urge to distance oneself from convention and achieve the majesty of a personal style.

Naturally, that often unrecognized freedom of modelling oneself, by oneself and primarily for oneself, in the mode of a moveable feast of self-construction, is not exempt from the highs and lows of fashion or the cruelty of the whip; but self-definition, and the emancipatory panorama that opens up beyond what it seems one possesses – mere subjection to the current vogue

– often has need of the mirror of others, requires imitation, the shaking-up and turning-around of imposed models, sometimes at the cost of pain and absurdity, in order to finally arrive at a 'oneself', a one of many and possibly ever-more personalized reinventions.

In every era, the wig has also landed on heads as an affront, an apparently frivolous short-range subversion of a marmoreal notion of identity. In place of the rigid styles that tethered hair and bound women to a social position; in place of lacquer that sets it into a sober, respectable monolith (no way is it going to come loose and precipitate the feared stampede of the emotions), the wig is complicit in a more fluid, defiant conception of the I, in which hair, that indomitable quantity which has to be tamed each day as if it were a wild beast, becomes the password for movement, the hirsute mirror of the transition between mental states, the talisman of regeneration.[*]

After the at times scandalous wig of ancient Rome, women continued to have recourse to substitute tresses as a conduit to the recovery of self-esteem, an exorcism of dissatisfactions or an effective magic formula for vanishing conjugal monotony. In Paris and London, both historical capitals of the modern wig, their diffusion followed a downward hierarchical path from the pinnacle to the people, in a denaturing of the symbol that, while retaining elements of emulation and aspiration, opened windows to the dream, who knows if marmoreal or horny, of being what one desires.

~~~~

[*] Due to its astonishing change after flowering, the shrub *Cotinus coggygria* 'Royal Purple', whose habitat extends from southern Europe to the Himalayas, is popularly known as the Wig Tree, but also the Smoke Tree.

Gillette Elvgren, *Gentlemen Prefer . . . ?*, tintogravure of painting, 1963, advertisement by Brown and Bigelow, Inc.

The wig, an all-too-human substitute for the animal crest, confers the capacity for change, prepares the way for a predicament that exceeds the merely external. In spite of being a mere addition, the borrowed mop of hair very soon integrates into the psychological plot the unfinished jigsaw puzzle of the person wearing it; less a simple prosthesis than a missing piece, less a luxury than the restitution of yearnings, the hairpiece is that personal, some would say minimal contribution to the patchwork of inherited rituals and constraints that underpin identity, that touch of artifice which, albeit almost floating in the air, indicates the ideal of personal reconstruction.

From an early age Marguerite de Valois, who became queen of Navarre following her marriage to Henry III, supplemented her dark mournful locks with magnificent blonde wigs made from hair cut from the heads of pageboys employed expressly for that service (according to the *Encyclopédie Diderot et d'Alembert*, the best samples came from countries where cider and beer were drunk). In England, where the origins of the rage for wigs are still debated, there is evidence that as far back as the reign of Elizabeth I their use was fairly common, and that she herself used to wear one to hide her baldness, then considered a deformity. During her life she achieved a respectable collection of several hundred models, all reddish in colour. Her chromatic preferences caused a commotion and soon the streets of London were ablaze with the saffron locks of her plebeian impersonators.

Elizabeth's cousin Mary, Queen of Scots, was also attracted by the magnetism of self-aesthetization, although she did not suffer from alopecia and her hair follicles in fact seemed up to their task. Her preference was for silken, chestnut curls, which came to be a mark of monarchical elegance. While there is no evidence that the spirited rivalry between the two women had hairy origins (and as far as is known they never tugged at each other's pigtails), when Elizabeth ordered the beheading of her cousin and enemy, in the midst of the general shudder when the executioner failed at the first blow and had to swing his axe

English School, *Queen Elizabeth I*, late 16th century, oil on panel; one of the more candid depictions.

François Clouet, *Mary, Queen of Scots, c.* 1558, miniature watercolour on vellum.

again, the astonishment of those moments in which the cloth of reality seems torn prevailed: when the possibly still live head was raised, at the instant when the executioner cried 'God save the Queen', its locks came loose. The discovery of her grey, thinning hair was like a double decapitation. Due to its metaphorical power and the suddenness of the revelation, all eyes were fixed on the inert hair, forgetting the bloodied head. Was that unexpected unmasking, that proof of a penchant for falsity and show (according to some historians this is nothing more than a gore myth), perhaps a punishment added to the well-publicized execution?

Despite the taste for wigs having spread like wildfire throughout the British Isles, the commotion in the square suggests that rather than an innocent piece of coquetry, a ruse for concealing the signs of ageing, the public understood the wig as fraud, a compromising act of duplicity, as if the Scottish queen 'not only harboured falsity in her soul but also on her head'. After being tried for her participation in a plot to assassinate the queen of England, Mary Stuart was marked by the suspicion that simulation and changefulness engender, by the crime of having been convinced, like so many other women – among them Elizabeth herself – that the body is not irrefutable proof, an entity in itself, a datum.

Long before the invention of twenty-minute dyes and the perms that replaced ringlets, before the advent of the excesses of cosmetic surgery and silicon implants, the wig was preparing the way for that intimate revolution – a revolution more contagious than many others, although towed by the imperatives of ownership and social pressure – thanks to which a change in the body could bring about a change in life.

As an insignia of the transitory body, a direct route to remaking the sense of identity and a prop in the *mise en scène* of that identity, the wig was one of the seeds of malleable self-creation, the standard of that radical turn in the politics of the body that, on confining biological inheritance to a mere first draft from which to reinvent oneself, an unfinished medium for coupling with what is to come, makes artifice a form of resistance and a (not just cosmetic) path to liberation, a repeal of the sentence of having no other mask than one's own face.

Andrés de Castillejos, *Jesús Nazareno de Cádiz* (*El Greñúo*), 1590–1602.

Devotional Hairstyles

In the silent shadows of a church, more chilling than the stigmata or the cross itself, hair thrives like sucker fish on the effigies. I shall never forget the childhood spell that seemed to draw my eyes to those animal, mortuary excrescences. How is it that I can conjure up from the corners of memory, where they have been floating like dust or fluff, those lugubrious strands, strewn on pillows, all too vivid and Medusa-like, capable of eclipsing any religious mystery? In a space where symbolism had been reduced to zero and the body (one of its most infamous components) appeared in its crudest conclusiveness, the transubstantiation was for me absolutely unimportant.

In contrast to the pagan fertility rituals in which a woman had to choose between the sacrifice of her locks or ritual prostitution with strangers (Mediterranean children were also shaved at puberty as a tribute to Adonis, Apollo or Asclepius), today there are still many believers who offer up their tresses in the no less outlandish ritual of dressing saints (a tradition, not exclusive to single women), which is deeply rooted in Andalusia, where the Virgin of Hope of Macarena sports a metre of human hair and the statue of Christ, with its wig of natural hair, is known as *El Greñúo*, the man with tresses. As a gesture of humility and renunciation, a possibly stentorian vow of chastity, the sacrifice of hair could be said to carry the issue to the least appropriate location, where women must cover their heads with shawls or mantillas and where wearing it loose is a sinful variety of nudity.

As a faithful image of the life force and fertility, hair has always been a half-drawn curtain behind which lies sex. In the temple to Venus Calva (the bald Venus) in the ancient Roman Capitol, the locks sacrificed to the goddess were intended to ensure both offspring and good harvests (due to its regenerative powers and a morphological similarity to stems and roots, hair has ever been associated with the vegetable kingdom). Not long afterwards, in Catholic churches, its control signified a step towards purity in which the strength of the desire for renunciation is confirmed by a covered head or, in the case of men, a tonsure.

Although there is no clear evidence of what was actually done in antiquity with the greater part of that strange votive mass, that hirsute pile suddenly become sacred, stories do exist of warrior sacrifices in ancient Rome in which the offering-up of hair to Mars was not merely a metaphorical act: it was employed to plait the string of the bows used in battle. The fact that many years later those ceremonial remains adorn statues of saints in churches seems to point to some form of syncretic tangle and perhaps remnants of idolatry. Without ever attaining the status of relics, in Catholic statuary that hairy debris is located further up the hierarchy than the wood or plaster – materials for representation, for the continuation of martyrdom through an effigy – in a flagrant abandonment of any attempt at mimesis. In the same premises where blood is wine and the body of Christ is eaten on a daily basis, hair is simply, overwhelmingly, hair.

Both a bridge and a sluice gate between Hebraic tradition and Christianity, Paul of Tarsus insisted that an uncovered female head was a mark of dishonour and he hastened to establish rules for women's attire (1 Corinthians 10–11). He speaks of hair as a woman's 'glory', and long hair being given to her as a 'covering'. In order to avoid the capillary contamination of churches by the malevolent sensual power of curls, he even warns women against them with the fanatical zeal of one who understands that curves are suggestive, an unacceptable invitation to lewdness, forgetting that Jesus himself gladly let Mary Magdalene dry his feet with her locks. In an asymmetry that can be attributed to his desire to distance himself as far as possible from his Jewish upbringing, the apprentice rabbi and later saint finds no reason for concern in relation to men, and states that when they form part of the congregation, they should take off their hats as a sign of reverence. Goodbye to the kippah. The Devil, it would appear, does not make his nest in masculine hair.

In spite of the wig having some relationship to a covering (*supervestiri*), the severe apostle does not clarify whether he considers it to be a veil of modesty – even today a Jewish wife swears fidelity by its use. However, his restriction soon expanded to include it. Fearing hair's power for innuendo, even when its excess and lack of restraint is a pretence, the Church Fathers fostered the conception of the wig as an enemy of chastity and excommunicated it at each new council. To lend weight to their cause, to breathe strength and trepidation into their papal bulls, they had at hand the still living example of Roman licentiousness, which eased the passage of the dictum that adulteration is invitation to adultery.

That the wig enjoyed good health in the first centuries after Christ can be inferred from the number and variety of arguments used to revile it. Clement of Alexandria adduced that it was an obstacle to benediction: the sign of the cross made in the air as a blessing could not pass through the barrier of another's locks. Tertullian warned of the shadow of the Devil in an almost living article that, in the end, is an encouragement to falsehood and duplicity, and he did not hesitate to remind those most given to its use that they might be adorning their heads with the remains of an executed convict. Since it distinguished them from Jews and pagans alike, the followers of Jesus quickly expelled wigs from their households in preference for styled hair and tonsures. One might suppose that the eye of the needle leading to the Kingdom of Heaven shares certain qualities with a knife-edge.

Although female hair is indistinguishable from its male counterpart in strictly material terms (how often has the figure on the cross in a church been topped by a woman's mane?), the person wearing it and the way it is worn mark a difference in its erotic attraction. Whether due to its sinuous qualities, its animal silkiness or its wild disorder – not to mention its relationship to other hirsute areas of the body – it is not unusual for hair to participate in obscenity. Malleable even in the symbolic realm, one might imagine that a head of hair offered to a church is free of any form of sensuality, as if, once over the threshold, that aspect had been snipped off. Any hint of sacrilege would dissipate under the sacrificial blades of the scissors and, above all, under the pretext of endowing sacred images with presence and life; images that, unlike shop-window mannequins, even in mid-ecstasy, shore up the illusion of something that is not entirely of this world.

But once in its new avatar, exhibited in a glass sarcophagus or trickling like blood below the crown of thorns, devotional

Pedro de Mena, *Penitent Mary Magdalene*, 1664, detail of wood sculpture.

hair attains the realm of prohibition by way of the path of reverence and untouchability – the characteristic sphere of the corpse. Ready, even groomed to give substance to a simulacrum, the hairpiece is contaminated by the rigor and enclosure of death, and soon unlooses its sinister potential. It is no longer a material that enhances fertility but a herald of the ephemerality and decrepitude of all things worldly. In the manner of the skeletons of the *danse macabre*, whose incarnations of Death include long tresses and are living, unforgettable reflections of mortality, the curly-haired saints and Christ figures find us as unprepared for an examination of the conscience as for horror.

The Chimeric Wig

'If the mask is the face of dreams, the wig is the crown of nightmares.' This sentence cannot be found in Roland Topor's *Le Locataire chimérique* (literally *The Chimeric Tenant*), but it could be the epigraph to the novel or, even better, one of its unwritten passwords: the protagonist, Trelkovsky, a solitary man with no past, buys an expensive wig that makes him look like a ridiculous elderly prostitute in an attempt to transform himself into Mlle Choule, the previous tenant of the flat where he now lives, who had thrown herself out of one of its windows.

Although he had already taken possession of her clothes and cosmetics and followed her footsteps like a contented puppet, Trelkovsky rebels against the change of identity his neighbours seem to want to impose on him and seeks to free himself in the most inconsequential, grotesque manner by taking the initiative in the metamorphosis. In this way, he succeeds in transforming all his actions, the shuddering jolts more like those of a corralled beast than a docile animal, into a disconcerting form of passivity. On leaving a boutique – the wig shop requires that name – with a false head of hair softly brushing his face, he knows that he is just one step from becoming a stranger. He will no longer be the awkward tenant, that loud but ghostly presence who never really fits in, and will take on a feigned personality, a foreign but recognizable body that exorcizes oblivion by means of clamour and monstrosity.

In the building on the old-fashioned rue des Pyrénées, where keeping up appearances is still important, taking the place of someone else implies not only matching their habits – slipping back and forth like a shadow, smoking their brand of cigarettes – but a complete substitution, a change of sex included. For foreigners, as any newcomer knows well, sometimes the only way to integrate is by accepting the role of victim. Trelkovsky follows Choule's final steps like someone who has to learn a sacrificial dance towards the void.

Roman Polanski transforms into Miss Choule in *The Tenant* (1976), directed by Polanski.

In *Le Locataire,* Roman Polanski was able to make Topor's novel his own because in some way it also spoke of him. (Why else did he reserve the starring role for himself?) Rather than a screen adaptation, the duo of Polish Jews in Paris created a bicephalous work, half-novel, half-film, among whose themes are the condition of being the outsider, the need to assimilate, that urge to become transparent in order to pass unnoticed.

As if there were something intrinsically incriminating in his movements, as if he were guilty of being who he is, Trelkovsky/ Polanski becomes a nuisance for his neighbours, who would prefer him to lead the silent, exemplary life of a mummified corpse. No matter what he does or how many precautions he takes, as he moves through the flat his footsteps seem amplified, inappropriate, if not dishonest, marked by the unsilenceable creak of otherness. In one scene of intransigence and arbitrariness that would have brought a smile to Kafka's face, he is blamed for noisy comings and goings on a day when a burglar breaks in during his absence.

Spineless and discreet, an office worker who takes correct behaviour and amiability to the verge of distraction, Trelkovsky's first transformation consists of adopting the parsimony of a vulture: although he doesn't admit it to himself, he wants Choule to die so that he can take over her flat, and he makes this outcome more likely when he visits the hospital where she lies bandaged from head to toe and is received with a scream that mixes surprise and horror at the twists of fate. The Egyptian thread that runs through the book – there are hieroglyphics on the walls and postcards of tombs – culminates, as in the cyclical time of the pharaohs, in the eternal return of the same and Trelkovsky's conversion into a mummy: the same mummy who shudders at the sight of a discreet, foreign-looking office worker paying her a hair-raising visit in hospital, another turn of the screw in a real-estate torture of Tantalus.

Among Trelkovsky's many transformations, the most decisive is facilitated by the wig. The small flat, as claustrophobic as the grave, not only contains Mlle Choule's belongings, but her ghost; that is, the trail of her presence embodied in her clothes, the arrangement of the furniture and possibly in the vivid memory of her movements and habits. But dressing and making himself up like her is not enough to give a credible body to the fantasy and Trelkovsky, with the perplexed obedience of one who carries out a ritual that has to be guessed on the hoof, decides to behave like a lost piece of a jigsaw puzzle, aware that the edges do not match up: he settles a conjectural head of hair over his own and extracts the same tooth the woman is missing, as if employing age-old symbols of identification and disguise – hair and teeth – were the final step in being accepted by the neighbours. As with other acts of cross-dressing, he is not seeking a precise reconstruction but the reproduction of an *effect*, the same one that, however, he did not manage to achieve through the personal effects of the former tenant.

His state of being both a stranger and foreigner and the cogwheels of paranoia draw him inexorably towards the morbid pleasure of gratifying the long-standing residents of the building and yielding to their unfathomable designs. In response to their perverse vigilance, their plot to change him into someone else and then annihilate him, he produces his own aberration. The idea of buying the wig marks the moment when he completely loses his head. That is his secret rebellion: to speed up the metamorphosis, make it his own, a twisted rather than lifelike

Michael Caine as Dr Elliott's alter ego, Bobbie, in *Dressed to Kill* (1980), directed by Brian De Palma.

escape route. If being accepted in the building requires the renunciation of his identity, he will show them what he is made of. Wearing the gleaming wig, still tottering in high-heeled shoes, he practises speaking in a falsetto tone before the mirror, gracelessly swinging his hips. 'Beautiful, beautiful, adorable, goddess, divine,' he says in an inevitably off-camera voice, with a borrowed, unconvincing smile, on the point of falling over the edge into the absurd.

Due to its complexity, the abundance of symbols – lost teeth, the accumulation of rubbish, shit delivered to his door, voyeurism, doubles – since its premiere in 1976, *The Tenant* has been the delight of psychoanalysts. As was the case earlier with Hitchcock's *Psycho* (1960) and later with De Palma's *Dressed to Kill*, the ritual act of cross-dressing leads to the defiles of insanity. There is, however, no need for a grand hermeneutic barrage to notice that the discordant, riotous wig on Trelkovsky's head is not entirely an adaptive or mimetic measure; as a narrow passage to the shadowy zone of the split personality, it is in fact the ostentatious crest of his rebellion. The displaced man is not disguising himself as Mlle Choule, nor is he fantasizing about changing sex as a repressed urge, but is supplanting that urge in his body and destiny; he is her predictably exaggerated replica. In reaction to the disproportionate pressure from the neighbours, he could have accepted being the obedient, silent *locataire* who eventually achieves the invisibility of the perfect tenant, but he prefers the defiant route of stridency. Always on the point of being thrown into the street, always on the verge of having no place in the world, he chooses to throw himself, in woman's clothing and a wig, into the abyss the others have reserved for him.

That Old Camp Stridency

Whatever happens to hair seems to be projected onto the whole body. In Margo Glantz's *De la amorosa inclinación a enredarse en cabellos* (On the Amorous Inclination to Get Tangled Up in Hair), the author states that 'hair is a rigorous metonym.' Letting one's hair down, freeing it from combs and pins, has been an expiatory form of unbuttoning; an invitation, at once a red carpet and a rope ladder, of the variety Rapunzel extends from her tower. On the other hand, uncombed hair, when not a declaration of principles in which forms of rebellion come together in a ravelled thread, suggests a certain degree of desperation, sometimes ruinous isolation: having no one to 'watch our backs', to smarten us up, urge us, comb in hand, to contain the disaster that has taken over our heads.

The signs of the wig are variable and changeable, crossed by equivocation and the simulacrum, but its tangled semantics often include the desire for mutation, an irreverent refusal to accept, even if only partially, inherited appearance, the genetic burden and the hairstyle imposed by parents. In contrast to the notion of naturalness, in barefaced defiance of what is supposed to be immutable, artifice can be the suspension bridge to another dimension of the self, where identity is understood as an endless quest, and the moulding of what we want to be entails care of the 'look' and getting it completely wrong.

As a communal cypher that does not escape the heights of fashion, a falsifiable password that allows us to cross determined bridges and be part of a fraternity, an always revocable form of self-design that puts us in a position to be hard on the heels of current modes, capillary grooming is less a vehicle for keratinous effusion than one of the main referents of generational change, an eloquent symbol of the gap between us. Whether loose and ruffled, or with the gelled perfection that could be called 'aspirational', the zeitgeist is sculpted in hair.

The wig, which is allied to all things androgynous but can also underscore gender codes, which has been the insignia of exaggeration and the supremacy of effect, is a decidedly camp item of dress that celebrates the inappropriateness of things and contributes to shoring up the metaphor of life as a stage. In her notes on that form of sensibility in which affectation and imitation come into play to the benefit of the fantastic, Susan Sontag does not directly mention hairpieces, but she considers them as part of that passionate and ingenuous excess whose only intent is to aestheticize the world. *Démesuré* and *démodé*, the two French words that best express the sense of camp, are ideal for describing a taste for wigs, a taste that has throughout history been stigmatized as frivolous and superfluous, and this despite the fact that, possibly due to the vivacity of its hedonism, its struggle with shallowness, the hairpiece has been so necessary in various eras.

If, as Sontag says, camp is the response to the problem of 'how to be a dandy in the age of mass culture', then, based on its synthetic elaboration, the wig once again bursts onto the scene. From Baudelaire's blue model to Elton John's capillary eccentricities, or the polished immoderation of the nineteenth-century

Dusty Springfield wearing a beehive wig on the set of the *Thank Your Lucky Stars* TV series in Aston Studios, Birmingham, 1966.

dandizettes to Dusty Springfield's curled or Cher's stunning locks, fake hair has kept alive the attraction of the non-natural – of the supernatural as a path to personal affirmation – and cleared the way for the discovery of the liberating qualities of 'bad taste', grossness, failure and even kitsch, which can then no longer be simply disdained.

A peroxide blonde from the London suburbs, an ugly duckling who made artificiality the new face of glamour, Dusty Springfield was the curious queen of camp who, with a crepuscular voice whose range easily descended to the male register, took on the tautological, overcharged role of the hyper-woman. With just a few tools to hand – heavy eyeliner, red lipstick, miniskirts made from curtain material and wigs enlarged beyond the realms of possibility by the use of spray – she constructed an audacious, brazenly fake image that drank from the spring of 1950s cinema divas and the decadent charm of drag queens, who, in an endless play of mirrors, would soon be imitating her and incorporating her into their shows.

A contemporary of the Beatles and conscious of the importance of capillary provocation in music, of the idea of 'artisticness' in every gesture, in the smallest details of appearance, Dusty took the leap that would allow her to draw a line on her past as an innocent child who sang traditional music with her family and start covering African American songs, second-hand versions of blues hits, exploding racial stereotypes of authenticity and ownership.

As the 'White Lady of Soul', whose role models were Bessie Smith, Billie Holiday and Nina Simone, and who located her vocal entertainment within black culture, in her subversive style she sowed the idea that circumstances of birth are mere accidents, that it is possible to reinvent oneself to the rhythm of one's desires. And then, to the unashamedly camp cry of 'the lie that speaks the truth', she left behind the ordinary Mary O'Brien, that obedient convent-school girl, to mutate into something much more than a superstar: the unlikely icon of self-transformation.

Due to the genial fearlessness with which it opposes the prevailing seriousness, its sometimes involuntary if not ingenuous humour inspired by vaudeville and farce, it is often believed that any explosive capacity camp might have has been deactivated:

as if the almost parodic blade that it uses to slash at pigeonholes were nothing more than a stylistic device, the ephemerality of a pose, practically devoid of commitment and ultimately banal. Sontag herself took its depoliticized or apolitical nature as a given . . . but rather than a style without further implications, a mere positioning of the gaze, camp is capable of including an impulse towards transgression and the undermining of hierarchies. Although in certain aspects it has been integrated into the category of queer, camp, through its exaggeration and extravagance, has succeeded in making it clear that in the formation of identity opposites are just deep-rooted conventions, possibly not so innocent simplifications, and that if one wants to avoid making the self a definitively prefabricated doll, an embittered, anaesthetized puppet of society, as corresponds to the most complex of artifices, it is essential to take charge of the formation with one foot in the conviction that, as Oscar Wilde wrote, 'to be natural is such a difficult pose to keep up.'

As a simple means of dodging compartmentalization, of riddling monolithic, crystalline notions of identity with holes, and even for forays into noise and fright (as is the case of Copi's old transvestites in the story of the same name – 'Las viejas travestis' – hilarious heroines of hyperbole and parody, but also of what is irreducible and transgressive), the wig has also had a certain indomitable if not explosive profile, as if an unexpected stick of dynamite were waiting at the end of its colourful tresses.

If imitators dressed in drag-queen style have paid tribute to Dusty and continue to offer her new life to the wrap-around rhythm of 'Son of a Preacher Man', this is due to that fact that at the height of her career, with her sexual orientation always under suspicion, she embodied the critique of social binarism,

Bert Errol posing for a portrait in drag, 1930. Born Isaac Whitehouse, he was one of the most successful female impersonators in British music hall. From 1910 until 1921 he also made frequent appearances in big-time American vaudeville.

Harris Glenn Milstead, known by his stage name Divine, in the 1972 John Waters film *Pink Flamingos*.

the strict divisions articulating the logic of exclusion, beginning with black and white, native and foreign, genuine and fake, homo and hetero. With their self-confident affront to the male/female division, not to mention the recursive play of original and copy, drag queens added to the questioning of the body as a sort of random, genetic calamity – a description already dynamited by Dusty and other outstanding figures, not only in the music world – dissatisfaction with established models.*

As the diva fetish of drag, at once sombre and dazzling, with that velvety voice ideal for expressing discontent and disobedience, for voicing that discontent to a world she would never completely fit in with, she should be recognized as the person who, within the realm of popular culture – within the heads of thousands of young women who followed her example – shattered the notion of identity as an unequivocal given, of the body as an unalterable ready-made.

---

* In relation to camp politics, Harris Glenn Milstead, better known as Divine, the actor and singer of John Waters's craziest films, should be remembered not only for his non-stop carnival, his cult of dissonance and the transvaluation of bad taste for which he was a standard-bearer, but as a complex and indefatigable defender of human freedom, of the reinvention of the self that does not shrink from monstrosity.

The Tangled Mop of Fetish

Jealously guarded by psychoanalysis, claimed as its own by anthropology, the word 'fetish' is one of the most elusive in the lexicon. As if every attempt to corral it or tie it to a precise or 'true' meaning only strengthened its resistance, its gentle but obstinate slippage, on the verge of transforming itself into the great fetish of thought, it would appear to be a word coated with the slime of over-interpretation, by layers and layers of abuse and equivocations that ultimately show how deeply it is submerged in the swamp of ambiguity.

Nevertheless, there is hardly any other object – and this book might be the irrefutable proof of it – so closely linked to fetishism as the wig, with its social significations and ability to arouse intense personal obsessions. As the fabric of appearance and symbols – systematic imposture and a weapon of destruction, anomalous merchandise that can be mistaken for a natural fibre – the wig lends itself to being taken as a precise illustration, requiring only a few theoretical contortions, of the phenomenon of fetishism in its anthropological, psychoanalytical, politico-economic or simply colloquial senses.

A duplicitous article of clothing, the wig may be helpful in understanding the adoration of the object in its unquestionable materiality, that enchantment aroused by natural bodies before they have reached the point of participating in, as Kant insists, the Sublime, or as Hegel would have it, the Idea – and, therefore, History: a situation in which, according to these thinkers, locks of hair and other articles found themselves on the west coast of Africa at the end of the sixteenth century, at the dawn of the practice of *fetiço*. But the wig can also be seen as a crystallized, libidinous yearning, as that 'unfit substitute for the sexual object' Freud refers to, whose fixation originates in a strong impression during infancy, typically at the moment of becoming aware of the difference between men and women in terms of castration. For its part, the head of hair fabricated to disguise baldness or extend capillary attributes slots easily into the Marxist theory of the commodity: it is no longer a simple magical object that acquires social value in primitive societies, but a manufactured article that masks the social relationships of exploitation and, as if it were indeed in some way 'possessed' (*dixit* Marx), seems to have a life of its own and enjoy a phantasmagorical will, a suprasensible power that situates it above its producers and users, who end by coveting and to some extent sanctifying it.

The list of illustrations could go on and on with a wig appearing from the top hat of the various theoretical positions. It could be evoked as, for instance, the perfect vignette of Jean-Paul Sartre's 'detotalized totality', William Pietz's syncretic fragmentation or even as one of those loci of mystery mentioned by Gilles Deleuze and Michel Leiris, through which sanctioned social objects come to be experienced as embodiments of values or virtues – and, ultimately, as carriers of power.

Otherwise, from an etymological viewpoint, the mop of borrowed hair would seem ideal for the elucidation of the term. 'Fetish' is derived from *facticius* (a made thing, fabricated), and it scarcely needs to be stressed that the Latin root is also related to the artificial, false, unnatural quality of the object, and is coincidentally associated with its power to embellish, the charm that springs from its interior; in Spanish *hechizo* (witch-craft) and fetish share the same linguistic origin and form a thread in which false hair is entwined with sorcery and where the vehemence of obsession borders the supernatural.

In dictionaries the fetish is often compared to a form of idol or a primitive cult of effigies. Yet rather than an autonomous statue, a complete, recognizable universe that functions as a pretext for fascination, the fetish points towards something frag-mentary, partially dismembered or broken, which in its origins is expressly fabricated to be worn, to hang from and be added to the body like an amulet, and which in its popular accepta-tions still involves a variant of metonymy, a certain system of transposition which, in taking the part for the whole – the detail for the entire body – carries the risk of falling into a powerful form of psychological repression.

It was precisely that fragmentary, concentrated and detailed nature of the fetish that led Severo Sarduy to relate it to a pic-torial effect, to that form of partial illumination known as *caravaggismo*: 'The brutal projection of light – a summary pro-cedure for attracting the gaze – which is concentrated on one part of the body.' The excessive, at times monstrous, attraction of a particular aspect; the eroticization of an area of the body brought into focus – an area that is often fantasized as detach-able, or even, disgracefully, amputatable – or of part of its clothing, extensions or prostheses, has the effect of casting a shadow over or displacing everything else (the person and sur-roundings included) towards the nadir of disinterest, the blackness of flaccidity, in a play of light and dark, of sectarian emphasis, which also includes the oppositions of alive and dead, the pulsating and the frozen, erection and deflation.

If I resist locating the wig decisively on the side of the fetish, it is because in the various representations of the phenomenon the string of difficulties and precautionary measures for battling with what is so different, so other that it can only be stigmatized as irrational, are as clear as an inescapable, incriminating black thread. The fetish is an all-purpose concept for approaching the incomprehensible, all that is opposed to the rigid grid of Logos, the unconscious complexes of infancy . . .: the fetish as a demarcation of the boundaries of the unthinkable.

First, the figure of the savage as the embodiment of 'the other', that inhabitant of the west coast of Africa who clings to some extraordinary talisman and, through a process that appears to have neither primitive nor natural laws – 'just prior to History' – organizes his desires and beliefs around a form of worship that is barely distinguishable from witchcraft. But something similar occurs in the psychoanalytical focus on fetishist fixation as 'unfit' desire, that is, as disorder and deviation (and in the end, as an illness), the effect of the void perceived by the male psyche on becoming aware of gender differences. And even Marx, in his mannered 'The Fetishism of Commodities and the Secret Thereof' in *Capital*, finds no other recourse than to describe communist fervour by use of enigmatic images that refer directly to mysticism and seem more reminiscent of a diabolical possession in which commodities are filled with chimeras, suprasensible qualities, and sprout phantasmagorical wings that, over and above their use value, make them dance in the collective imaginary, charged with a repressive bewitchment.

In 'A Tress of Hair', Maupassant describes the stages of a macabre, erotic capillary mania in which, after a particularly sharp delimitation of desire, only madness can be expected. The story, which feels like a compilation or synthesis of the main assumptions related to fetishism, tells the tale of a wealthy collector whose passion for antiquities takes on certain sensual and carnal overtones. Driven by an almost painful need to possess, he buys an old Italian cabinet in which he later finds hidden 'an immense coil of fair hair, almost red, which must have been cut off close to the head, tied with a golden cord'. Despite the passage of time, the overwhelmingly alive and suggestive hair – a veritable *invitation au voyage* – gradually takes over his dreams and drives as if something of the soul of the owner had been trapped in it.

The substitution, the triumph of the strange synecdoche is completed in gradual but increasingly strong spasms of pleasure and pleading, but the day comes when that stream of hair serves as a real woman, as maddening and sensual as she is cold and tyrannical, whom he loves uncontrollably, whom he passionately kisses, burying his lips in her hair, even taking her to a box at the theatre as if she was his wife.

The story, the first in a gloomy, eccentric series that seems to have no other connecting idea than a devotion to Poe and Baudelaire, prepares the way for a decadent form of literature where eroticism is inseparable from morbidity, and in which unknown pleasures, always located in the ranks of mental unbalance, become entangled with melancholy and even death through the fatal rites of barely glimpsed masturbation. In both Georges Rodenbach's *Bruges-la-Morte* (Bruges Death) and Efrén Rebolledo's *Salamandra*, hair is not only the cursed trophy of an impossible, ill-fated love, but, thanks to the disturbing

Michel Piccoli in the short film *La Chevelure* (1961), directed by Adonis Kyrou and based on the short story by Guy de Maupassant.

materiality of the object of veneration, also the predictable noose of hangings in which sexuality scarcely intervenes. Elena Rivas, the aloof and naturally irresistible femme fatale of *Salamandra*, weaves the web of her masterpiece with the poisoned chalice of her hair. In a white velvet box that accentuates the blackness of the soft, scented treasure it holds, she sends the poet Eugenio

León – the most reckless and vulnerable of her admirers – not so much the substitute for what he will never taste as the instrument with which, once the bewitchment of the fetish has become a form of torture, he takes his life in the most artistic way imaginable. He himself has already prepared the scene on publishing a poem, the last verse of which reads:

> And your dark hair is a heavy shroud,
> a funereal bracelet; but its fascination
> is so great that, making a noose from its strands,
> I would kill myself with its murderous silkiness.

In contrast to Rebolledo's novel, which among other things proclaims the morbid lack of satisfaction offered by the fetish, it has been suggested that Maupassant's story gives a key to understanding the mechanisms through which a dead body can be converted into an object and, more importantly, a cult object (Michel Serres dedicates a whole chapter to this in his book *Statues*). For my part, I would like to point out that the story is also a vivid, highly insightful portrait of the ease – not to say facility – with which society applies the mythology of rationality to phenomena it does not understand, to outlandish behaviours it refuses to condone, displacing them towards the margins of perversion, superstition and morbidity. Guy de Maupassant, himself hounded by hallucinations and plagued by insanity during his final years, chose to open his story in an asylum, in a cell of isolation and punishment that, seen from the perspective of a container which has escaped sanity and its norms, seems to be a sign of the incomprehension and stigma with which we have historically treated the fetish.

A Knife Named Guillotine

At the peak of elegance, understood as an investiture rather than an extension of the vestment, as a shameless crowning ornament of wealth and power, the decadence of the wig came tumbling down to the cry of 'Liberty, Equality, Fraternity'. That strange entity which is not quite an article of clothing or an accessory, that takes root in the individual psyche despite being added and detachable, might nowadays occasionally provoke a short-lived party mood and an impoverished fantasy of freedom, but has generally fallen into disrepute as an instrument of oppression, an all-too-ostentatious reminder of injustice.

The beginning of the end was in gestation long before the storming of the Bastille, possibly from the time when the practice of powdering wigs became an unsustainable fashion, a hypertelic squandering bordering on insult and tactlessness. In his 1807 general history of hairpieces, Friedrich Nicolai locates the first example of the whitened wig on the stage of the *comédie*, from which it dispersed like a fragrant cloud to embellish both men and women (there is, however, some evidence that the emperor Commodus adorned his with gold dust and aromatic oils). During the seventeenth and eighteenth centuries, the application of a fine dusting of flour was a daily ritual of the aristocracy, and special rooms were set aside for just that

Philibert Louis Debucour, after Carle Vernet, *La Toilette d'un clerc de procurer*t, 1816, engraving. A prosecutor's assistant has his wig powdered by a barber, his face protected by the long cone he is holding.

purpose. The procedure, which was so laborious that it required the assistance of a hairdresser (or lackeys with a talent for sprinkling that somehow magical powder), allowed the hair to be tinted with such unusual colours as pink, lilac and blue, and saturated with intoxicating perfumes and essences, no small matter for the recherché French sensibility. The favourite vegetal preparations were violet water and a concoction made from rose petals, cloves and lemon peel. Although the scent of hair can be seductive, the mix of sweat, exotic extracts and fermenting flour must have produced the somewhat less intoxicating sense of nausea.

As might be expected, a problem arose in the form of a shortage of bread; when farmers' scales were weighted towards satisfying the taste for luxury and vanity of a few, ignoring the needs of the many, the extravagance of the fashion began to have a high political cost. In spite of Louis XV's 1740 ban on the use of edible flour for such frivolities as hairdressing (according to Baudelaire, the king had carried his depravity to the point of only being able to enjoy 'simple nature'), the practice was by then so deeply embedded that it continued come hell or high water, even during the reign of his successor; in contrast to the English situation, the decree did not specify offences or involve any form of taxation.

Popular unrest at this squandering of flour was so widespread that it would be no exaggeration to see the wig, if only allegorically, as one of the sparks that detonated the Revolution. Marie Antoinette's famous reply to the people's demand for bread – 'Let them eat cake!' – might not, as the legend goes, have lit the insurgent fuse (apparently it was an old joke that had been doing the rounds at Versailles for decades), but the prevailing atmosphere of inequality and scarcity cannot be ignored, and would explain, among other things, the queen's sobriquet: Madame Déficit. In his *Tableau de Paris*, Sébastien Mercier calculates that 200,000 heads were subjected to the habitual rite of powdering, each one covered in a curious conical mask. Following his reasonable arithmetic, those kilograms of rice and wheat flour would have fed 10,000 hungry citizens for a year.

If the wig is, among many other things, a *symptom*, a form that expresses 'the psychopathology of affluence' (Sontag), it should be no surprise that the republican band saved their most brutal acts for the overloaded heads of the monarchy and their outlandish hairstyles: to be strictly logical, the infallible blade of the guillotine also dethroned the wig, put an end to its curly conceits, annihilating in a single swipe its long reign, the class differences that it had supported during the old regime with a wealth of insolence and luxury.

But if the wig *also* brought about a radical change in hairstyles – failure to come to terms with the new atmosphere of austerity and one's own hair was considered unpatriotic and carried risks – and while the National Convention of 1792 officially abolished it as a throwback to another time and a counter-revolutionary provocation, this measure did not pass unopposed, and many Jacobin leaders refused to abandon their old attire and habits. In 1793, the year of Marie Antoinette's execution, when, as legend has it, half of Paris watched not only her head, but the compromising letters concealed in the structure of her hair tumble from the platform, numerous Jacobins were still conspiring with their long wigs blowing in the winds of change (although many of them wore uncurled models of natural colours) and there is evidence that Robespierre, alias *The Incorruptible*, turned his back on the general disapproval and, unconcerned about the semiotic charge of his appearance, never renounced the controversial talcum.

That scarcely a year later destiny would catch up with Maximilien Robespierre in the incontestable verdict of a metal blade cannot only be put down to personal appearance; in those convulsive years when wearing the austere attire of the sans-culottes was a motive for pride and a political vindication, a lack of simplicity in attire could well have fatal consequences. Although, in his speech of 5 February 1794, Robespierre called for 'the rule of reason for the tyranny of fashion', he failed to show any great disposition to overthrow the tyranny of the wig, which is why so many historical tales and high-budget films insist on portraying him, even on the day of his execution, dressed in the shreds of his contradictory hairpiece.

After a few death rattles that at times made it seem almost alive, the hydra that is the wig, which had taken possession of millions of heads in Europe and the greater part of its colonies, was finally defeated. With it went a whole era, an age that de Musset summarized as 'starch'. The master wigmakers, an influential, affluent guild that in 1789 had 20,000 members in France alone, did all it could to save its cause, and launched sober, unostentatious models that even Rousseau would have approved of ... But to no avail. Their guilds were soon dissolved and their privileges removed. A very few, the most needy or obliging, reinvented themselves as well-known barbers at the service of the Revolution, more specifically the *rasoir national*, the rite of the blade to which those condemned to death were subjected. If any haircut, however inelegant, was enough to clear the throat of the inclemency of the guillotine, it was crucial for the executioners

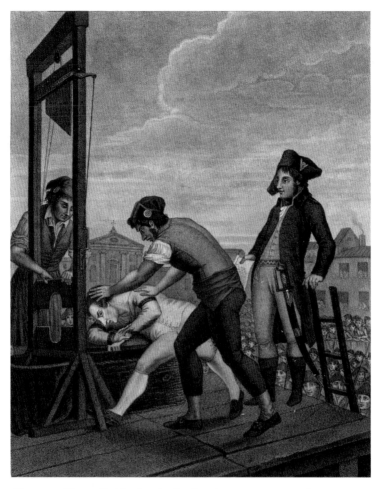

Giacomo Aliprandi, *The Death of Robespierre*, 1799, engraving.

to be able to get a firm grip on the head in order to display it to the onlookers.

From then onwards, from that shaven head sporting the wig as a covert crown, it entered a long, pronounced period of eclipse. With the exception of the British law courts and the theatre, where it still reigns as the queen of the wardrobe department,

A FRENCH HAIR DRESSER
Running through the Streets to his Customers
Publish'd According to Act March 1st 1771 by W. Darling Engraver in Great Newport Street

William Darling, *A French Hair Dresser Running through the Streets to his Customers*, 1771, satirical print.

the wig was confined to a secondary, anecdotal and shameful role, its only powder being the dust of oblivion of attics and chests, reduced to an outdated plaything, an unmentionable prosthesis, an obsolete curiosity for bouts of loose living that fizzled out before the party had ended.

But the fact that the wig is still alive, if only as an element of disguise or the desperate successor to the locks plucked from the scalp by age, heredity or chemotherapy, should perhaps be a motive for reflection and alarm since it indicates that times of change and rebellion are not at hand, that none of those historical upheavals that occurred at the height of its power are in sight.

If the decline of ancient Egypt began with an excessive penchant for the hierarchy of the wig; if the fall of Rome was hastened when marble statues started to wear interchangeable models and Caligula demonstrated his authority by a beard of gold and, finally, if the monarchy was abolished in France at the most Churrigueresque moment of its capillary display, then the renaissance of the wig could well be the beginning of a new end, an omen of a catastrophe of incalculable proportions. In the 1970s, when the rage for the pixie wig was at its height, just after the stylist Carita triumphantly reintroduced it on the catwalks for Givenchy's collection, *Vogue* editor Siriol Hugh-Jones warned that a fad for wigs normally precedes disaster, the fall of monarchs and governments, and blood running through gutters.

The Discourse of False Hair

I n the same way as Theodor Adorno suggested that slip-
pers are 'monuments to the hatred of bending down', the
wig is a register of more or less misguided gestures, behaviours
and expansions related to the metamorphosis of the self, dis-
simulation and a concern with keeping up appearances. If the
modelling of hair is one of the keys to the modelling of identity,
to that sculpting of the self about which not only beauty salons
but books of philosophy talk so much, it would seem natural
that the upper part of the head should become a battlefield, a
disputed territory into which the quest for belonging and indi-
viduality overflows, and where the generation gap is embodied,
at times in a sharp, strident form.

Salvador Novo, possibly the most shameless and genial
writer among the group known as the Contemporáneos, noted
in his 'De pelos y señales' (On Hair and Signs) that if we understand wigs as forms of refraction, as stand-ins for confronting
the caprices and accidents of nature, it has been women, those
whom one would initially say were least in need of them, who
have used them with the greatest imagination and sense of liberation. The hairpiece as an accomplice in the game of seduction,
a pocket carnival that highlights both the features and the fluctuating qualities of the self, went into notable decline for men at
the end of the eighteenth century, with its associated surge in

the use of cosmetics; even Novo, who had to wear a hairpiece for decades, was, with perhaps inconsistent modesty, careful 'never to mention the toupee' (a colloquial phrase that in Spanish roughly translates as 'No way!') although he at times dared to don models that matched his unashamed, picaresque style of writing: it is said that in his walks through La Lagunilla market in Mexico City he used to wear pink or blue wigs, and that on more than one occasion he turned up to read his poetry in a green hairpiece.*

But the discourse of hair (I am alluding here to an article by Pier Paolo Pasolini), that ancient *ars rhetorica* which reached a rarely seen peak during the 1960s with flowing locks as a declaration of rebellion and tribal nostalgia (a peak prefigured by the so-called Bearded Revolution), can be ambiguous and changeable even when the artificial does not intervene in its disordered syntax. While what Margo Glantz terms 'protest hair' (almost always linked to the songs that stand in for hymns) can be associated with hippy tresses soaked in patchouli and strewn with flowers, it would be just as reasonable to allude to the spikes worn by punks, and of course the dreadlocks of Rastafarians, conspicuous clans or ways of life that insist on carrying their demands firmly perched on the head. The fact that there is nothing to stop the location of that collection of rebellions in the gleaming quiffs of the *Grease* generation (whose

---

* It is often forgotten that in the late eighteenth century men were the pioneers of the use of cosmetics and elaborate clothing. When they renounced the wig, make-up, lace, heels, moles and hose for a neutral, acceptable sobriety, the male of the species deprived himself of half the game of appearances, the creative power of self-definition through grooming, an activity which, if it is not embodied in some way in the figure of the dandy, nowadays carries the stigma of effeminacy.

'Saturday night fever is the fever that hurls young people into respectability', the fever of the gallant and conservative values related to the American way of life) or many of the other fringes and haircuts that present themselves with a touch of high-sounding sensitivity, indicates not only that protest is relative and its liberating emblems mutable, but that the gunpowder of hair can be easily dampened by Vaseline, particularly when it is not attacking any given order, and in fact trivializes the impulse for protest through uniformity and predictability; when the sculpting of the I, the conquest of the self based on hyperconscious decisions that incorporate and transcend cosmetic effect, is accepted in a vein no longer of autonomy but as a product, subjected to standardizing parameters.

From the symbolic schoolboy castration of Isidore Ducasse, Comte de Lautréamont, which marginalized him to 'the expressive lack of hair' (in *Le Chants de Maldoror* he refers to the nightmare of a bald scalp, 'polished as the shell of the tortoise'), to the memoirs of the Rolling Stones' guitarist, Keith Richards, in which he relates the uproar caused by his hair during a tour of the southern United States in the mid-1970s and makes an observation that could be the epigraph of this book – 'Hair ... the little things that you wouldn't think about that changed whole cultures' – tresses have traced out an unmistakably noisy mauditism but also the rather ordinary arc of their media consecration: from the chosen appearance as otherness and provocation, where the head of hair is the ideal peak on which to unfurl the fan of affront, to its neutralization as a mere fashion, where the dissonance of the hair has lost its subversive potential and, automatically copied without knowing why, is reduced to the standard of a new form of servitude, another marketing variable.

Authentic Beatle wigs for only $2.99, advertisement in *Beatle Mania: The Authentic Photos* magazine, 1964.

What disconcerts Pasolini (and also Glantz) is the ambiguity of long male hair as an unarticulated system of signs. In the midst of the updated utopias and bucolic reveries of a generation, that non-verbal discourse tolerates the presence of intruders and provocateurs by the simple ruse of using long hair as a form of disguise, the handy recourse of adopting the mask of androgyny, of the fierce pacifist who has hardly heard of Rousseau. And in this way, rather than simply deactivating its signs, reducing hair to just another adornment, it succeeds in turning its reverie upside down and disrupting the unity between untidiness and insurgency.*

As if everything concerning hair, starting with discourse, spontaneously inclined towards entanglement, at the moment when some *outsider* decides to grow his hair, when even *insiders* noisily reject the Gillette (not because its design is reminiscent of the scalpel that influences and embodies its ordinariness, but because that act allows them to observe the insider codes), what hair seemed to be saying lost not only force, but resolve and clarity; those disgraceful mops of hair were no longer championing the rejection of consumer society and its conventions in terms of appearance; the scarecrows constructed like antibodies of hegemonic values suddenly display another profile and are soon promoted as the model for a new form of spectacle, as a compelling ideal of beauty – if it knows about one thing, it is keeping up to date – for which even nausea and disbelief are poses that can be perfected in front of the mirror.

* In the film *El mundo fantástico de los hippies* (The Fantastic World of the Hippies), with his inimitable mode of involuntary surrealism, Juan Orol tells the story of an undercover agent who, in order to complete his decidedly non-pacific missions, dons the duplicitous wig of peace and love.

If an excess of hair, with its irrepressible and 'natural' look, can change its symbolism and form part of the props for a cinema advertisement (and the box-office success of the rock musical *Hair* should not be forgotten), the gesture of wearing a wig, of trusting in artificial locks as a replacement that exceeds anything orthopaedics can offer, is always just a hair's breadth from becoming a flagrant misunderstanding. The fact that the last great historical season of wigs coincided with wild hippy hair, the unexpected re-evaluation of an untamed beard and proud armpits only muddies the waters. On emerging in the late 1950s from its prolonged hibernation, and against the grain of the natural, anti-cosmetic turn that was gathering steam during those years, it would seem reasonable that, as with the French Revolution, artificial hair and extensions would arouse every form of ill will and suspicion, and that sooner or later they would be surrounded by the aura of ruin and destruction their contagion tends to trigger.

But perhaps precisely because there were too many elements at play during the 1960s, because a hairy scalp become a surface for the projection of desires and widespread complaint was reaching saturation point, the wig did not establish itself in the imaginary as the indisputable sign of affluence and display. And despite women in particular adopting its use with a passion, clearing the way for the renaissance of spectacular Afro poufs and no longer baroque but by then Gogo locks, its re-emergence was tinged with a certain good-times frivolity, and its condition as a plaything was even exploited by advertisers. As a consequence of, among other factors, the low cost of synthetic fibres, which made it accessible to any pocket, the status of the wig plunged to being mistaken for a symbol. Once ideological differences were again being expressed through capillary conflicts, the distortion that false hair represented, with its burden of superficiality and simulation, made it inappropriate for an age that was all too conscious of its obligations, committed to the hilt to causes and principles flourishing on shaggy skin. Just when sideburns, beards, length or shagginess were beginning to have an openly political function, the wig's ephemeral and interchangeable nature could only be interpreted as flippancy, as the seal of fluctuating convictions and chameleonic passions.

Yet in the clamour of fashionable capillary discourses, in which no one could innocently neglect to use a hairbrush or sport an Afro without the act being seen as a proclamation, the role of the wig may not have been limited to elevating the sudden Babel of hair to new heights. Through the display of its own excess, of the brashness of its moveable feast, the wig highlighted the artificiality of those confrontations in which the various sides attempted to define themselves by hair, and where nonconformism and conformity, libertarianism and repression were basically measured by the comb and a pair of scissors, both of which are dangerously absurd scales.

If in other times (the English Civil War, for instance) the wig was capable of weakening polarization and easing the tensions expressed even through hair, during the rebellious, hope-filled years of the 1960s, when the discourse of non-violence was expressed in tresses and the military crew cut was a means of concealing hair that was standing on end, the resurgence of hairpieces contributed to the clouding of supposedly monosemous messages and served as an ironic contrast to outbreaks of follicular fundamentalism. Just as one can manipulate the

Advertisement for affordable Valmor wigs, 1970s.

Advertisement for Star-Glow wigs, 1970s.

attributes of manliness through stick-on patches of chest hair; just as the pompous, elliptical pretension of 'naturalness', of an appearance that has no time for effects and implants, is laid bare by the wig as another variant of vanity, simply one more form of swagger, so the temptation to do without verbal language, to overcome reasons and arguments through the mono-discourse of hair, finds its limit and a counterpoint, a denial and an occasion for scorn, in the duplicity of artifice, in the noble old simulacrum of the wig.

Bedside Reading

Barado, Francisco, *Historia del peinado* (A History of Hairstyles), facsimile edn (Valladolid, 2009)

Bornay, Erika, *La cabellera femenina* (Female Hair) (Madrid, 2010)

Cooper, Wendy, *Hair: Sex, Society, Symbolism* (New York, 1971)

Daguerle, J.N.M. (Dr Akerlio), *Éloge des perruques* (In Praise of Wigs) (Paris, 1799)

Futoransky, Luisa, *Pelos* (Hair) (Madrid, 1990)

Glantz, Margo, *De la amorosa inclinación a enredarse en cabellos* (On the Amorous Inclination to Get Tangled Up in Hair) (Mexico, 1984)

González Crussí, Francisco, 'Nuevo elogio de la calvicie' (A New Tribute to Baldness), in *Letras Libres* (February 2011)

Kwass, Michael, 'Big Hair: A Wig History of Consumption in Eighteenth-century France', *American Historical Review*, CXI/3 (June 2006)

Le Fur, Yves, *Cheveux chéris. Frivolités et trophées* (Beloved Hair: Frivolities and Trophies) (Paris, 2012)

McCracken, Grant, *Big Hair: A Journey into the Transformation of Self* (New York, 1996)

Monestier, Martin, *Les poils. Histoires et bizarreries* (Hair: Stories and Oddities) (Paris, 2002)

Nicolai, Friedrich, *Recherches historiques sur l'usage des cheveux postiches et des perruques dans les temps anciens et modernes* (Historical Research on the Use of Hairpieces and Wigs in Ancient and Modern Times) (Paris, 1809)

Novo, Salvador, 'De pelos y señales' (On Hair and Signs), in *Las locas, el sexo y los burdeles* (The Madwomen, Sex and Brothels) (Mexico City, 1972)

Pasolini, Pier Paolo, 'Il "discorso" dei capelli' (The 'Discourse' of Hair), in *Scritti corsari* (Corsair Writings) (Milan, 1975)

Pauls, Alan, *Historia del pelo* (A History of Hair) (Barcelona, 2010)

Rimmel, Eugene, *The Book of Perfumes*, facsimile edn (London, 2005)

Synesius, *In Praise of Baldness* (1985), available in English at www.livius.org

Thiers, Jean-Baptiste, *Histoire des perruques* (A History of Wigs) (Avignon, 1690)

Villaret, M., *Arte de peinase las señoras a sí mismas* (The Art of Hairstyling for Women), facsimile edn (Valladolid, 2006)

Woodforde, John, *The Strange Story of False Hair* (London, 1971)

Photo Acknowledgements

The author and publishers wish to express their thanks to the below sources of illustrative material and/or permission to reproduce it. Every effort has been made to contact copyright holders; should there be any we have been unable to reach or to whom inaccurate acknowledgements have been made please contact the publishers, and full adjustments will be made to any subsequent printings. Some locations of artworks are also given below, in the interest of brevity:

Photos Luigi Amara: pp. 18, 65, 202; © 2020 The Andy Warhol Foundation for the Visual Arts, Inc./Licensed by DACS, London: p. 74; Bibliothèque nationale de France, Paris: p. 235; Bodleian Libraries, University of Oxford: p. 105; The British Museum, London: pp. 85, 108, 129, 236; from Denis Diderot and Jean le Rond d'Alembert, *Recueil de planches, sur les sciences, les arts libéraux, et les arts méchaniques*, vol. VIII (Paris, 1771), courtesy Smithsonian Libraries, Washington, DC: pp. 22, 37; photo Fine Art Images/Heritage Images via Getty Images: p. 188; photo courtesy Jean-Claude Francolon/Gamma-Rapho via Getty Images: p. 180; Glyptothek, Munich: p. 97; photo Chris Hellier/Bridgeman Images: p. 100; photos Heritage Auctions, HA.com: pp. 114, 115; photo courtesy International Center of Photography/Getty Images: p. 67; J. D. Doyle Archives, Houston: p. 220; The J. Paul Getty Museum, Los Angeles: p. 174; Library of Congress, Prints and Photographs Division, Washington, DC: pp. 25, 78, 139, 165; from Ludwig Christian Lichtenberg and Friedrich Kries, *Georg Christoph Lichtenberg's Vermischte Schriften*, vol. III (Göttingen, 1801), courtesy ETH-Bibliothek, Zürich: p. 154; photo Philippe Lopez/AFP via Getty Images: p. 190; The Metropolitan Museum of Art, New York: pp. 12, 120, 126, 152, 160; Mozarteum Foundation, Salzburg: p. 90; National Gallery of Art, Washington, DC: p. 149; private collection: pp. 179, 198, 231; photo David Redfern/Redferns via Getty Images: p. 217; Royal College of